Chamberlain Association of America

Report of the Meetings for Organization and of the first General

Meeting

Together with the President's Address, and a List of Members

Chamberlain Association of America

Report of the Meetings for Organization and of the first General Meeting
Together with the President's Address, and a List of Members

ISBN/EAN: 9783744729611

Printed in Europe, USA, Canada, Australia, Japan

Cover: Foto ©Suzi / pixelio.de

More available books at **www.hansebooks.com**

Chamberlain Association

... OF ...

AMERICA.

Report of the Meetings for Organization and
of the First General Meeting, together
with the President's Address,
and a List of Members.

BOSTON, SEPTEMBER, 1898.

Chamberlain Association

. . . OF . . .

AMERICA.

Report of the Meetings for Organization and
of the First General Meeting, together
with the President's Address,
and a List of Members.

BOSTON, SEPTEMBER, 1898.

The Chamberlain Association of America.

FOR some time previous to and during the year 1897 representatives of the various branches of the Chamberlain family of New England had expressed a wish that steps might be taken to form an association for genealogical and social purposes.

As a result of the interest manifested, and particularly through the untiring efforts of Miss Abbie M. Chamberlain, of Cambridge, Mass., who had corresponded with members of the family throughout the country, and received most encouraging replies, a call for a preliminary meeting was issued. The call read as follows : —

BOSTON, October 25, 1897.

To MEMBERS OF THE CHAMBERLAIN FAMILY:

Dear Kindred and Friends: — During the past year a strong desire has been expressed among various members of the Chamberlain family that an organization be formed for social and genealogical purposes.

Among those in full sympathy with the proposal are ex-Gov. Joshua L. Chamberlain, Brunswick, Me. ; Judge Mellen Chamberlain, Chelsea, Mass. ; Rev. Dr. L. T.

3

Chamberlain, New York City; Hon. Daniel U. Chamberlin, Cambridge, Mass.; Col. Thomas Chamberlain, Philadelphia; Herbert Chamberlain, Brattleboro, Vt.; Dr. Myron Chamberlain, Boston; William S. Boynton, St. Johnsbury, Vt.; Edward W. Chamberlain, Louisville, Ky.; Rev. Henry E. Jewett, California; Charles Chamberlain, Rockford, Ill., and many others.

The proposal has been received with so much favor that the undersigned venture to call a meeting of such members of the family as can be reached to take the matter into consideration, and if deemed expedient to organize such an association.

We would name as the time and place of such meeting, Saturday, October 30, at 3 P. M., Room 13, Congregational House, Boston.

You are most cordially invited to be present at this meeting.

> DANIEL U. CHAMBERLIN,
> ASA W. CHAMBERLIN,
> E. E. STRONG,
> C. N. CHAMBERLAIN.

There were thirteen persons present at the meetting, which was called to order by Mr. Asa W. Chamberlin, who expressed great pleasure in being connected with the beginning of what promised to be an interesting movement. He then nominated Dr. Cyrus N. Chamberlain as Chairman of the meeting, who was unanimously elected. On taking the chair, Dr. Chamberlain expressed in brief but graceful words his warm interest in the movement. Miss Abbie M. Chamberlain was chosen Secretary of the meeting, and read extracts from various letters she had received from those who were unable to attend the present meeting, but who promised hearty support in carrying out the purposes of the organization.

After an informal discussion in which the majority of those present took part, it was voted to form an organization to be known as the Chamberlain Association of America. A committee was appointed to report a plan of organization, and another committee to nominate a board of permanent officers, both to report at a subsequent meeting.

The second meeting was held at the Congregational House, Boston, on Saturday, December 18, 1897, at which twenty-five persons were present.

Dr. Cyrus N. Chamberlain presided.

The Committee on Permanent Organization reported a form of Constitution and By-Laws which with some slight amendment was adopted.

The Nominating Committee reported a list of officers for the ensuing year, and these were elected.

General Joshua L. Chamberlain, LL. D., who was chosen President, upon taking the chair was given an enthusiastic reception, to which he made a brief but eloquent response.

On motion it was resolved that all persons who had joined the Association up to the present time — some fifty in number — should be considered as " charter members."

After the meeting had been formally adjourned, a pleasant hour was spent in forming and renewing friendships and establishing relationships, and thus the real work of the Association was at once entered upon.

During the following months six meetings of the Executive Committee were held, in which the future work of the several Standing Committees was discussed and preliminaries were settled for holding a general meeting.

That meeting, which was the first general assembly or reunion of the Association, was held at the Parker House, Boston, on Thursday, September 8, 1898. In the morning a business session was held,— the Committees having met at an earlier hour,— at which the President, General Chamberlain, presided.

The Secretary reported that the membership numbered one hundred, representing nineteen states and the District of Columbia, and sixty-two cities and towns.

The Treasurer submitted the accounts, which were passed over to the Auditors.

Considerable discussion was elicited upon several subjects which came before the meeting, but nothing of importance was determined except some modifications of the By-Laws.

In the afternoon, at 3 o'clock, a reception was

held in the parlors of the hotel, which was attended by about a hundred persons, members and their kindred, who spent some two hours in social and fraternal intercourse.

In the evening the goodly company sat down at a table beautifully laid in the banquet room of the Parker House — the whole effect of which was decidedly brilliant. After this natural expression of sociability was well fulfilled, the President introduced the feast of minds and hearts by some remarks which he was requested by an urgent and unanimous vote to put in form for publication under charge of the Executive Committee, who were deputed to send a copy to each member of the Association.

The President's address was followed by other speeches and interchanges of sentiment which sparkled with passages of wit and eloquence. Among the speakers were Generals Samuel and Robert Chamberlain, Dr. Cyrus Chamberlain, Miss Jessie Chamberlain and Rev. Dr. Strong. The speeches were interspersed with music by members of the party and by letters and telegrams from numerous absent members, who thus conveyed their regrets and congratulations.

REMARKS

MADE AT THE DINNER OF THE CHAMBERLAIN
ASSOCIATION, BOSTON, ON SEPTEMBER 8, 1898,
BY GENERAL JOSHUA L. CHAMBERLAIN,
PRESIDENT OF THE ASSOCIATION.

Companions and Kindred:

We are glad to greet each other in such numbers
and with such omens of good. Our date for this
first reunion finds many of our associates held away
from us in bodily presence by previous engage-
ments, or by circumstances of the season. Their
letters, however, give us the touch of hearts if not
of hands from far and wide over the country. And
from what we see around us, we are sure some
covenant of inherited blessing is fulfilled in us by
this high privilege.

This is a beginning. We look forward. Although
judged by the spirit of zealous research so manifest,
we seem to be concerned wholly with things that
are long past, and to measure our importance by
the distance to which we can dig up our roots in
that direction, the real motive and reason of this
association is the good we can do each other and
those who belong to us or with us, in the present

and future time. We are slender and small in some aspects, but our sources reach back to mighty things; and we propose to increase, both largely and richly, both in content and intent, for mighty things to come.

Much is said now-a-days about the descent and ascent of man. Science would curb human pride by assuring us that we are all descended — or I believe the word ascended is permitted — from the simian tribe, whose previous best effort or efflorescence is the anthropoid ape. I should say of this introduction of new relations, as President Lincoln said to the book-agent, "For people who like that kind of a book, that is just the kind of a book they would like." To those who are pleased with this proffer, we extend our entire consent, and yield them the ground. "Similia similibus." But "similia simiis,"— we are not "in it." The Chamberlain family claims descent, no doubt, from an upper story; but we do not look for our forebears in the trees. Our first parents made rather poor work of it under them. They doubtless looked up to these wonderful beings,— parodies or paradoxes of themselves,— without envy, as they reached down to them hanging in inverted order by extension of the inferior back-bone. That relation we recognize; we like back-bone; but we prefer ours all to ourselves, and brain-end up! The new claimant to old priority has one set of locomotors the advantage of us. If he can overtake us, he is welcome on his arrival; but we will not run back after him. We will even help him to be the best possible type of his kind he can; just as we are doing for other remote fellow creepers or climbers, near and far, over the seas, or half-seas-over!

This talk about ascent and descent is very much a play upon words. Strictly speaking, there is no up and down. Things go straight forward on their own lines, unless some outward force or inward weakness bends them from it. Although we are now told that what we call straight lines are in reality curved lines, respondent to some other force than the impulsive, and that the motions of the whole universe are a returning to its goal; so for us, there is no ascent nor descent except as towards or away from the moral truth in our natures, as in the universe; all of which have their life and law in God. And the hope, the glory and joy of our career is to get back where we came from,— richer in content, indeed, counting work as worth, having gained other talents, and bringing our sheaves with us; having justified our powers and possibilities by keeping faith with them under whatever tests. And what are these ideals of the soul,— these visions and longings which draw us to something seeming so deeply our own? Are they beckoning lights ahead? Or broken memories, or appointment and impulse given aforetime? How is it that this very "before" in place means behind in time? We march forward to get homeward. And the dream of returning is the song of the exiled soul.

That commanding reverence for ancestry in some races of the far East may seem to us like superstition. We are familiar with certain forms of it in the faiths of old Egypt and Greece and Rome. Something of it is seen in all races, and its strength is by no means in proportion to their dullness of spirit. This deep sentiment in the finer minds of China and Japan interests us because of its source in what we may call their metaphysics,— their peculiar Buddhistic conception of the nature of the soul, regarding it not as single, but as composite and complex — the necessary result of manifold thought and action of previous lives innumerable. This is something quite beyond and different from the doctrine of "transmigration of souls." This is a little better, I think, than to ascribe the soul to previous determinations in chemistry and molecular physics, as some modern masters in science insist.

But is there not, after all, something like this Oriental notion in our conception of the growth of character,— not confusing this with soul? Do we not see that character is largely the resultant of almost infinite imperceptible vibrations from all worlds with which we are in relations, traversing our spirits and leaving their impress? Hence we are so careful about environment. We know, too, that we are complex. We live in each other. Our sorrows and our joys reach beyond our single selves. Personal sacrifices and triumphs do not find their full accounting in the individual subject, but are related to a continuity and oneness of life in which each is dimly conscious of the whole.

We reject the Oriental belief because it impairs moral identity and responsibility; but we recognize the fact that the soul is subject to some kind of relationship, and that there is a mysterious continuity through parentage. The ancient laws of peace and war recognized a certain mutual responsibility among members of one family; and I am not sure but we ourselves do so, on the small scale if not on the large. And the mystic enhancement of power in the mother's bible and the father's sword brings out a new law of values not known to political economy or to any physical law whatever. Hence we are careful, too, about heredity, and have reasons enough of our own to justify that reverence for ancestry which characterizes these meditative races of the East.

The law from Sinai recognizes the covenant of the generations. But it is grounded on far different reasons from the metaphysical. The sanctions,—

the motives, certainly,— presented to us rest almost entirely on physical conditions and practical consequences. This law enjoins filial reverence as a condition of length of days, and the peace and prosperity they betoken and make effective. This was given as a law for nations; regarding the honor of the family and the sanctity of home as the basis of human society. No doubt obedience to this commandment on the great scale has had more striking vindications than appear in the mere individual. And I wish our nation would take heed that the loss of reverence is the loss of integrity of soul, making way for inroads of alien and evil forces that would turn aside the true inheritance and cut off the natural course of blessing. It is a safeguard of life to have something to honor, to reverence, to hold sacred and keep unsullied.

We hold, therefore, that honorable lineage is a rightful presumption and guarantee of character. And the habitual cherishing of such a thought tends to make it an active power for good, as incentive and guide of conduct, in whatever sphere or service. Hence we study to learn more of our origin, with assured faith that we shall find something honorable in it, and something making for nobility before us as well as behind us. We associate ourselves by token of a name. But names stand for things. They serve to mark, if not the essence or central idea, at least some striking peculiarity of objects, whether this be a feature, action, attribute, office or locality. A name is certainly something more than a number — a mere mark of separation; it is also mark of characteristic identity.

In our case the name betokens an office, and one of trust and responsibility. In our day and language it has some applications that confuse its significance. But its historical origin is clear, and of singular interest. Deep-colored threads of manifold history are woven into it. Its etymology makes manifest that it has come to us through the French, and also that it has taken on a German impress; while we recognize in the substance of the word the Latin, or perhaps older even than this, the Greek "kamera," the word for chamber, the radical idea of which is a vaulted place. This Latin form remains in Spanish, Portuguese and Italian,— "camera" or "camara." We also have the direct Latin word in English, with rather limited application.

But what kind of a lingo is this which makes the derivative "camarlingo", in Italian, "camarlengo" in Spanish, and "camerlengo" in Portuguese? How got in here that old High German *lenc*,— itself a curious compound, the *l* denoting frequency and the *enc* or *ing* marking some personal relation to the thing signified by the main stock word,—

as here, an attendant of the chamber; in what station, whether high or low, being determined not by the word but by its associations, in social and even political conditions? The overreaching Germans had taken this word camera from the conquered Southern peoples, and at a time when it already showed two marks of the popular transformation which since produced the languages of southern Europe known as the Romance, as is seen in the Pompeiian inscriptions in the first century of the Christian era. The short, unaccented vowel in the penult syllable disappeared, and a final unaccented vowel also disappeared, or was represented by a mute *e*, whatever the original vowel,— that poor little knock-about unaccented *e*, so easily dropped when you didn't like him, and so easily made to stand when you wanted something which wasn't much! This would give "camr"— a combination the German could not get over so easily as he could the Rhine, so took for a ferryman that easy-going *e*, and put in another *m* to make him stay there. This makes the German word "kammer," and putting on to that the *lenc*, makes the old High German derivative, the feudal "kamerlenc," later becoming "kämmerling." This word the conquering Germans bore back to the Mediterranean shores, where we see it taken up by the Southern tongues each in a fashion of its own. Early in the Provençal we find it quite German, "camarlenc," and soon "chamarlenc,"— prototype of our own "chamberlain."

This shows how the letter *l* with its final syllable got into the word. But how did the letter *b* get in — a letter nowhere appearing in the Southern or Northern forms of the word, but which in French strangely comes to take the place of the middle *e* in them? This gives us a look at the effect of local cross-currents on a passing language. The mighty outflowing of dissolving Rome flattened down with its own *débris* and spread to discharge itself by more mouths than the Tiber or the Po, the Rhone or the Rhine. First to the street Latin; then taking its way by forces of nature more than by military or political direction, or anything in the will of man. This "camera" was tossed about among the differing dialects of repeopled old Gaul, some of which, as the Provençal in the South, and the Picard and speech of the Ile de France in the North, did not tolerate the junction of the *m* and *r* brought about by dropping the intermediate *c*, as we have seen, in such spoken word as "camra"; and by a physiological "law,"— in which physical geography and psychic race-tendency had no doubt their part,— required the facilitating flux of the letter *b* to help mix these liquids to suit them. So we find in these dialects, for instance, "cambra" (Provençal), and "cambre" (Picard).

16

But what about this *ch* at the beginning, with a new sound, neither Latin nor Spanish,— unheard of before? We have remarked the occasional form "chamarlenc" in the old Provençal. This heralded what became a settled "law" in French. It is well known that in this language the initial *ca* of the Latin is replaced by *ch*,— usually attended by the softening of the *a* into *e*; as in the familiar instances, "cheval" from caballus, "chef" from caput, "cher" from carus, "chez" from casa,—"chez moi,"— house of me,— at my house. But observe that when this initial comes before two consonants, the *a* stands, not changed into *e*,— as in "charme" from carmen. And in the Isle of France, where was brewed the modern French language, this law of the *ch* prevailed.

And observe the reflex influence of this upon the German. For that great king of the Franks,— who in the fifth century gave the name to France,— this thoroughly German Emperor, with his capitals at Aachen and Ingelheim, this Karl Magnus, was to the Trouveres of France, "Charlemagne." Reciprocally, in old High German of even earlier days, we find "chamerlinc" grafted from the French.

At length the law of language was reversed. Or rather, alien forces which could not affect the vital law of birth came to determine what finished form should have most vitality and power. The election of Hugh Capet, Duke of France,— meaning then

17

only the region tributary to the little island on which Paris stands,— to be king of all the turbulent provinces scarcely held together under Charlemagne himself, made all those provinces France, and Paris their capital; and this set in motion the causes which made the dialect of the little Ile de France prevail over those of Normandy and Picardy in the north, and Burgundy in the east, and in the course of events overcame the beautiful language of the south — the Languedoc, the Provençal of the Troubadours,— and made itself once for all the French Language.

So we have our name accounted for: the stuff of it from old Rome; fused in the reactions of race and circumstance; forged and welded beneath the thunder-blows of Goth and Frank and Hun; baptized and tempered in the fire-flooded fields and weird smithies of Northman and Saxon; emblem of trusted office in the appointments of feudal courts old and wide as the empire of Charlemagne; brought at last to England by the Normans mingled of so many bloods. Hence its place in the literatures of all races taking manly part in the evolution of modern history. The track runs red, with love or blood, through all the story.

I have tried your patience. You will smile to be informed that you have been spared much: hence you may pardon me one or two reflections.

It is not a pleasant suggestion that words — or rather, the users of them — show a tendency to descend from their nobler signification to the lower and less worthy. Is it that the nobler ideas decline with what we call the advance of civilization? But it is worthy of note that this name of ours has strangely held its dignity. In Rome, in early ages of the Church, the camarlingo was treasurer of the Pope, chief of his staff, and in his absence president of the Holy See. In Venice the Camarlinghi were treasurers of the Republic in the days of her ancient glory, as the beautiful palace near the Rialto testifies today. In Spain, up to the time of the kings of Arragon, the courtly name and office held high place together, and the name held it when the office had gone, "cased in cedar and wrapped in solemn gloom." The German only among modern tongues, as if doubting the service of this "lenc," has braced up its imperialism by the punctilious "kammerherr."

The idea of trust and guardianship reaches naturally to highest associations. It was said of old, "Seest thou a man faithful in business," that is, in affairs of trust, "he shall stand before kings." The modern applications of the word in English return to the original Roman office, — the quæstor, guardian of the public funds, who opened and closed the treasury, where too were kept the standards of the

Legions. If the treasure-keeper does not hold his ancient honor with us, it is because we have made treasures of lower things.

It is surely an "augmentation of honor" that this name, rooted deep in Latin, and growing up and out with imperial Rome and empires succeeding and exceeding, should have held its integrity through all the vicissitudes of times and peoples and lands and tongues. Is it too much to infer that those who bore it bore it well? It may be that the associations of the name have a reflex influence on consciousness and character.

High-sounding, too, are these names in themselves,— a matter not to be passed over as trivial,— in all the tongues of that age of chivalry and state:

> "Whose muse, full of high thought's invention,
>   Doth, like itself, heroically sound."

Now for a few minor things to lighten our strain. We find the name in all spellings at a very early time,— among others, exactly as we have it, "chamberlain," in the French writers of the times of the crusades, and in the "middle English" of that day the spelling "chaumberlein." The present French form, "chambellan," is the very same, only assimilating the liquids *l* and *r*, making *ll*,— the *l* sound drinking up the *r*.

Amusingly enough, or possibly to mortify our worldly pride, and keep us back from "presumptuous sins," the word "cambrelan" in modern colloquial French is applied to a lodger who lives in one chamber. The word, you will remark, is not a true French form. It has the letter-form of the provincial Picard; not that of the princely Ile de France. But whether it marks one who can afford to have a room to himself and not in common with others, or one who can afford only a single room and not a suite, we accept the issue. In the former case it distinguishes one who would preserve personal delicacy and self-respect; in the other, it suggests the honesty that refuses to live beyond its means,— the honor that scorns to live a lie.

Fair as has been the lineage of the name, I have not found the persons representing it unworthy. Some there doubtless have been who have fallen short of their mark; some who have failed to obtrude their merit or perhaps their rights; some who have calmly suffered injustice, more from proud reticence than from meekness; some punished for the misfortune of being found on the right side at the wrong time. Of such obsolete religion, doubtless, most of them, as to prefer others to themselves; but waiving this virtue when manhood is called to the field of arms. The crusader's cross and scallop-shell and palmer's branch on so many old armorial bearings prove that they were not unheard of in Holy Land.

No names of theirs are found on the list of the 72,000 "sturdy beggars" hung by Henry VIII, Head of the Church, as the lesson of political economy illustrating his reign, or yet among the lines of ennobled favorites, endowed by spoils of suppressed monasteries and schools; but finding other exaltation wherever right is to be maintained or wrong cast down, when their line is ended with the halter, the axe, or the faggot, strangely out-ranking the sword!   It matters not much :

> "Whether upon the scaffold high,
>   Or in the battle's van,
>   The noblest place for man to die
>   Is where he dies for man."

But it is not needful to die in order to be noble. It is well-doing that deserves the guerdon.   And for this the opportunities were never more ample, nor more worthily met than now.   Nor has our name lost prestige nor our blood lost color.   In England, in America, in India, in Armenia, in Hawaii, and Japan, and the islands of all the seas, the name stands not indeed for ministers to kings, but for ministers to man.   And I am bound in truth to say that I have found the women of this blood singularly true and brave and strong of soul;

needing no complement nor duplication to make them more than ministers,— representatives and examples of what is noblest in manhood. One need but look on this assembly,— on this list of membership,— to comprehend what royal office is in these days committed to man in the guarding of treasures and the fulfilling of trusts. And if we discern the signs of the times, we see what place there is yet for names to be written high on the rolls of the world's redeemers: where not by "deeds of bold emprise," then, in whatever calling, by strenuous soul, outgoing love, outgiving worth,— steps and hands leading Godward!

LIST OF MEMBERS.

September 8, 1898.

(Those in heavy-faced type are "charter" members; those marked with an asterisk are dead.)

ACTIVE MEMBERS.

Col. HENRY H. ADAMS,	New York, N. Y.
Mrs. MARTHA E. AUSTIN,	Roxbury, Mass.
Mrs. E. S. BARTLETT,	Evanston, Ill.
Mrs. Ellen E. Blair,	Dorchester, Mass.
Mr. William Boynton,	St. Johnsbury, Vt.
Mrs. J. S. BROWNE,	La Grange, Ind.
Mrs. Mary C. Burnham,	Putnam, Conn.
Mrs. GEORGE M. BROWN,	Hartford, Conn.
Mrs. J. M. Brant,	Weymouth, Mass.
Mrs. CARRIE M. BUTTS,	Newton Centre, Mass.
Mrs. Sophia A. C. Caswell,	Cambridge, Mass.
Miss Abbie M. Chamberlain,	Cambridge, Mass.
Mr. Allen Chamberlain,	Winchester, Mass.
ALLEN H. CHAMBERLAIN, M. D.,	Foxcroft, Me.
Miss ALICE CHAMBERLAIN,	Hyde Park, Mass.
Mr. Asa W. Chamberlin,	Jamaica Plain, Mass.
Mr. CHARLES A. CHAMBERLAIN,	Westford, Mass.
Mr. CHARLES E. CHAMBERLIN,	Roxbury, Mass.
Mr. CHARLES K. CHAMBERLIN, *died*,	Pittsburg, Pa.
Cyrus N. Chamberlain, M. D., *dod*	Andover, Mass.

24

Mr. CHARLES W. CHAMBERLAIN,	Dayton, Ohio.
Mr. C. W. CHAMBERLAIN.	Boston, Mass.
Hon. Daniel H. Chamberlain, LL. D.,	
	West Brookfield, Mass.
*Hon. Daniel U. Chamberlin,	Cambridge, Mass.
(Died June 15th, 1898.)	
Mr. Edward Watts Chamberlain,	Louisville, Ky.
EDWIN A. CHAMBERLAIN, M. D.,	Trenton, N. Y.
Miss Ella J. Chamberlain,	Cambridge, Mass.
Mr. ELVORD G. CHAMBERLAIN,	Montclair, N. J.
Mr. EPHRAIM CHAMBERLAIN,	Medfield, Mass.
Mr. EUGENE C. CHAMBERLAIN,	Chicago, Ill.
Mr. EUGENE TYLER CHAMBERLAIN,	Washington, D. C.
Gen. FRANK CHAMBERLAIN,	Albany. N. Y.
Mr. FRED W. CHAMBERLAIN,	Montclair, N. J.
Mr. F. W. CHAMBERLAIN,	Three Oaks, Mich.
Mr. GEORGE R. CHAMBERLAIN,	New Haven, Conn.
Mr. George W. Chamberlain,	Weymouth, Mass.
Miss GERTRUDE CHAMBERLIN,	Boston, Mass.
Miss HELEN CHAMBERLAIN,	Andover, Mass.
Miss HELEN CHAMBERLAIN,	Hyde Park, Mass.
Mr. HENRY R. CHAMBERLAIN,	London, England.
Mr. Herbert B. Chamberlain,	Brattleboro, Vt.
Miss ISABELLA S. CHAMBERLAIN,	Washington, D. C.
Mr. Jacob Chester Chamberlain,	New York, N. Y.
Rev. JAMES A. CHAMBERLIN,	Newark, N. J.
Mr. JAMES ROSWELL CHAMBERLAIN,	Rochester, N. Y.
Miss Jessie C. Chamberlain,	Boston, Mass.
JOSEPH E. N. CHAMBERLAIN, M. D.,	Easton, Md.
Gen. Joshua L. Chamberlain, LL. D.,	
	Brunswick, Me.

J. P. CHAMBERLIN, M. D.,	Boston, Mass.
J. W. Chamberlain, M. D..	St. Paul, Minn.
Miss Laura B. Chamberlain,	Cambridge, Mass.
Miss Lizzie F. Chamberlain,	Cambridge, Mass.
Miss Lizzie Chamberlain,	Providence, R. I.
Rev. L. T. Chamberlain, D. D.,	New York, N. Y.
McKENDREE H. CHAMBERLAIN, M. D.,	Lebanon, Ill.
Hon. Mellen Chamberlain,	Chelsea, Mass.
Mr. Montague Chamberlain,	Cambridge. Mass.
Myron L. Chamberlain, M. D.,	Boston, Mass.
Mr. Newell Chamberlain,	Cambridge, Mass.
Miss N. A. Chamberlain,	Auburndale, Mass.
Rev. N. H. CHAMBERLAYNE,	Monument Beach, Mass.
Mr. ORVILLE T. CHAMBERLAIN,	Elkhart, Ind.
Mr. PRESCOTT CHAMBERLAIN,	Chelsea, Mass.
Gen. ROBERT H. CHAMBERLAIN,	Worcester, Mass.
Mr. ROLLIN S. CHAMBERLAIN,	Wilkesbarre, Pa.
Gen. Samuel E. Chamberlin,	Barre Plain, Mass.
Miss Sarah P. Chamberlin,	Salem, Mass.
Col. Simon E. Chamberlain,	Washington, D. C.
Col. Thomas Chamberlin,	Philadelphia, Pa.
Prof. T. C. Chamberlain, LL. D.,	Chicago, Ill.
Miss S. Emma Chamberlain,	Cleveland, Ohio.
Mr. S. T. CHAMBERLAIN,	Derby, Conn.
Mr. Thomas Chamberlain,	Hyde Park, Mass.
Mr. WILLARD N. CHAMBERLAIN,	Watertown, Mass.
Prof. WILLIAM B. CHAMBERLAIN,	Oak Park, Ill.
Mr. William Carlton Chamberlain,	Louisville, Ky.
Maj. WILLIAM N. CHAMBERLAIN,	Washington, D. C.
Mr. WILLIAM PORTER CHAMBERLAIN,	Knoxville, Tenn.

Mr. WILLIAM S. CHAMBERLAIN,	Cleveland, Ohio.
Mrs. T. EATON CLAPP,	Manchester, N. H.
Mrs. ALICE GERTRUDE C. CLARKE,	Southbridge, Mass.
Mrs. MARY L. C. CLARKE,	Andover, Mass.
Edward Cowles, M. D.,	Waverley, Mass.
Mrs. COYDON CRAIN,	Jamaica Plain, Mass.
Mrs. AMIE WHITING DAMON,	Reading, Mass.
Mrs. HARRIOTT A. FOX,	Chicago, Ill.
Mrs. Caroline W. Furst,	Bellefonte, Pa.
Mrs. Helen Guilford,	Minneapolis, Minn.
Mrs. O. H. HARDING,	Allston, Mass.
Miss Louise H. Hinckley,	Cambridge, Mass.
Miss CHARLOTTE A. JEWELL,	Hartford, Conn.
Mrs. Etta F. C. Kendall,	Auburndale, Mass.
Mrs. Eliza M. C. Kennedy,	Watertown, Mass.
Mr. Horace Kennedy,	Watertown, Mass.
Mrs. Harriet P. Kimball,	Dubuque, Iowa.
Mrs. HELEN M. CHAMBERLAIN LLOYD,	Andover, Mass.
Mrs. S. B. McLEAN,	Pittsburg, Pa.
Mrs. FLORENCE CHAMBERLAIN MOSELY,	
	New Haven, Conn.
Mrs. Carrie A. C. Oxford,	Elliot, Me.
Mr. George Herbert Perry,	Cambridge, Mass.
Mrs. Minnie A. C. Perry,	Cambridge, Mass.
Mr. Ralph Dana Perry,	Cambridge, Mass.
Mr. JOHN L. RINGWALT, Jr.,	Mt. Vernon, Ohio.
Mrs. C. W. Seymour,	Hingham, Mass.
Rev. E. E. Strong, D. D.,	Auburndale, Mass.
Miss Jennie Chamberlain Watts,	Madison, Wis.

ASSOCIATE MEMBERS.

Mr. GEORGE M. BROWN,	Hartford, Conn.
Mr. GEORGE B. CASWELL,	Cambridge, Mass.
Mrs. ANNA GARLAND CHAMBERLAIN,	Andover, Mass.
Mrs. ASA W. CHAMBERLIN,	Jamaica Plain, Mass.
Mrs. EMMA B. CHAMBERLAIN,	Chicago, Ill.
Mrs. FANNIE E. CHAMBERLAIN,	Philadelphia, Pa.
Mrs. NEWELL CHAMBERLAIN,	Cambridge, Mass.
Mrs. ROBERT H. CHAMBERLAIN,	Worcester, Mass.
Mrs. THOMAS CHAMBERLAIN,	Hyde Park, Mass.
Mr. JAMES H. KENDALL,	Auburndale, Mass.
*Mr. FRANK W. PERRY,	Cambridge, Mass.

(Died June 20th, 1898.)

LIFE MEMBER.

Mrs. LUCY D. CHAMBERLAIN,	Windsor, Vt.

Chamberlain Association

. . . OF . . .

AMERICA.

44294

Report of General Meeting

HELD IN

BOSTON, AUGUST, 1899.

Presented by
The Chamberlain

CYRUS N. CHAMBERLAIN.

Chamberlain Association

. . . OF . . .

AMERICA.

Report of General Meeting

HELD IN

BOSTON, AUGUST, 1899.

berlain Assoc. of America,

Oct. 11, 1900.

The Chamberlain Association of America.

ANNUAL MEETING OF 1899.

THE second annual meeting, reunion and banquet of this Association took place at the Parker House, Boston, on Wednesday, August 30, 1899.

The members of the Association began gathering about 10 o'clock, and the first hour was occupied with greetings and congratulations, and a conference of the various committees.

At 11 o'clock the members were called to order by the President, General Joshua L. Chamberlain, LL. D.

The Recording Secretary, Mr. Asa W. Chamberlain, read the record of the first annual meeting, which was approved.

The Corresponding Secretary, Miss Abbie M. Chamberlain, read her annual report, which is of great interest, both as to the encouraging facts contained therein, and the happy manner of its preparation. The report reads as follows : —

3

Nearly a year has rolled round since The Chamberlain Association held its first public reception and banquet in the Parker House, Boston. It was such a marked success socially that all voted to hold a reunion this year.

This Association had an honorable birth, in an unexceptionable environment, with worthy sponsors; for the first two meetings were held in the historic room thirteen of the A. B. C. F. M., in the old Congregational House on Beacon Hill, Boston. There were thirteen members met in that room thirteen, and, after listening to encouraging letters from distant Chamberlains, voted to form this society, with our noble President, General Joshua L. Chamberlain, at its head, supported by able Vice-Presidents. Like the Joshua of old, he has proved a most acceptable and successful leader, for in a little more than ten months, on September 8, 1898, we numbered one hundred on our roll-call of members. We have struck the note of progress this year by an increased membership; the society has not aimed at rapid growth, but to associate a body of men and women, congenial in aim, tastes and sympathies, who might enjoy social intercourse and unite in tracing out the Chamberlain genealogy.

We have found a pleasant comradeship in genealogical work, which has developed a kinship of thought and feeling along the same line. The

4

pendulum is swinging backward and the subject of genealogy is now coming to the front, since it is found that the study of patriotism and loyalty, in connection with ancestors, brings home those virtues with increased force and power, when they are our own "kith and kin," and it is not done to foster foolish pride and ambition. Military records, local histories and family traditions reveal the heroic character of many of the early Chamberlain settlers, and a large number of names are inscribed on our American Revolutionary records in New England, and are also prominent in later wars. Loyalty and Patriotism have been characteristic of the Chamberlain family as a whole.

We are indebted largely to two members of our society for the Report of the last Annual Meeting, and The Chamberlain Manual, containing the President's address, photograph, and a list of our members. Messrs. Asa W. and Montague Chamberlain are entitled to much credit for the able manner in which they accomplished the work. All will be much gratified to have the delightful address to peruse in their homes, while others can make the acquaintance of the President through his photograph. A copy of the Constitution and By-laws also has been sent to every member of the society.

On this year's roll we include members from two additional states, Alabama and Colorado, and are becoming international through a link in India and a member born in Peru, South America, but now resident in Colorado.

We record with sorrow the loss of three of our members by death. Mrs. A. G. C. Clarke of Southbridge, Mass., sister of Mr. Montague Chamberlain of Cambridge, died on July 8th. All of our members will tender their kindliest sympathies to the brother and aged mother of eighty in this bereavement, as well as to Miss S. Emma Chamberlin of Cleveland, Ohio, in the loss of her only brother, Mr. Charles K. Chamberlin of Pittsburg, Pennsylvania, who died on May 14th. Upon July 18th, another member, prominent in this organization, passed away, Dr. Cyrus N. Chamberlain of Andover, Mass. He was a charter member, the first Moderator of the society and the Chairman of our Executive Board of Management. We all feel his death to be a personal loss and shall miss his wise counsels, encouraging words and kindly interest in this Association. Appropriate resolutions of sympathy have been sent to his wife, family, and brother, Dr. Myron Chamberlain of Boston.

We miss the presence of our esteemed Treasurer, Mr. Thomas Chamberlain, to-day, for he crossed the Atlantic ferry for a change of air and scene, but will soon return, we trust, with renewed health and strength. Our Assistant Treasurer, Mrs. Caswell, has proved a remarkably good business woman, and brought out a good surplus again this year in our Treasury. She has done so well we shall have to make her service a life one.

The Chairman of our Genealogical Committee, Mr. Jacob Chester Chamberlain of New York, is planning a vigorous campaign, as will be seen by his report.

We sympathize with the Chairman of American and Colonial History, Dr. J. W. Chamberlin of St. Paul, for he writes that " he sits in sackcloth and ashes to-day because he cannot attend this meeting." We commend his motto, *"Spes et Fides,"* to the society.

We acknowledge with thanks the receipt of a beautiful volume entitled, "John Adams, the Statesman of the American Revolution, and Other Essays," by Judge Mellen Chamberlain of Chelsea, Mass., the Librarian of the Boston Public Library for twelve years and a Vice-President of this society, but unable to be present to-day on account of ill-health. All should visit the Chamberlain Alcove in the Public Library and see the American Historical collection presented to the Library by our respected colleague.

Mention should be made here of several publications received during the year — a booklet of poems by Mrs. Annie E. Smiley; short sketches of

7

General Joshua L. Chamberlain, of General Samuel E. Chamberlain in his old Barre home, and of Captain O. T. Chamberlin of Indiana; a history of the famous One Hundred and Fiftieth Regiment of Pennsylvania Volunteers by its leader, Colonel Thomas Chamberlin; a literary review by Mrs. H. P. Kimball; a leaflet on the Maine Indians and a Vocabulary of the Maliseet tribe by Montague Chamberlain; and the Memoirs of the late Mrs. Bloomer of Iowa by her husband, D. C. Bloomer, Esq.

We are glad to learn that so much interesting Chamberlainia is being issued by our members. The outlook for the future of the society seems remarkably hopeful.

We close with greetings to our distant members and a welcome for the new ones to this society and to old historic Boston.

Respectfully submitted,
ABBIE MELLEN CHAMBERLAIN,
Corresponding Secretary.

The financial report was presented by the Assistant Treasurer, Mrs. Sophia A. Caswell, a summary of which will be found on page 55.

The Committee on Genealogy, through its Chairman, Mr. Jacob Chester Chamberlain, presented the following report:—

This Committee has felt somewhat weighted with the responsibility that, mainly through its efforts, one of the objects of this Association must be carried on,—that of fostering an interest in the genealogy of the families surnamed Chamberlain (including all variations in the orthography of the name).; and also, that it will be expected to present, from time to time, records and gleanings which may interest the members and also encourage further research.

Ours is a family which traces its origin in this country, not to any one immigrant ancestor or original settler, but to several who are known to have been immigrants; and it may be well to here give a list and brief statement of the earliest records relating to them.

FRANCIS CHAMBERLAIN came to Virginia, in 1621, on the ship "Marmaduke."

HENRY CHAMBERLIN first appears in Hingham, Mass., in 1638, having come there from Hingham, Norfolk County, England, on ship "Diligent."

RICHARD CHAMBERLIN is first known as of Braintree, Mass., in 1642, being referred to thus in Boston town records of that date.

THOMAS CHAMBERLAIN first appears at Woburn, Mass., in 1644, where on May 29th he was made a Freeman by the General Court.

EDMUND CHAMBERLAIN first appears at Roxbury, Mass., in 1647, where on January 4th he married Mary Turner.

WILLIAM CHAMBERLAIN first appears at Woburn, Mass., in 1648, where on January 6th he was admitted an inhabitant of the town.

The Committee have proposed to designate as heads of families or branches only those Chamberlains known to have been in this country before the end of the seventeenth century; also those who may have come here later, provided the records actually show them to have been the original settlers of that branch or family line.

We, however, find many of our members tracing their ancestry to others than in the above-mentioned list; such as,

JOSEPH, of Colchester, Conn., about 1700.
LEWIS, of Amwell (now Flemington), N. J., soon after 1700.
THOMAS, of Talbot County, Maryland, soon after 1700.
JACOB, of Roxbury, Mass., in 1714.
WRIGHT, of Eastern Pennsylvania, about 1780.

Some of these branches may have been traced to their arrival in this country, and as soon as we receive these records, they will be classed as among the heads of families or branches.

During the past year, the Committee have received the private Genealogical Records of those members of this Association who have filled out the usual application form, and many have been classified under the heads given above; but in the absence of further dates and information, it has been a difficult matter to link the majority of members under any head. We find many trace their line back to the same ancestor, but of such comparatively recent date, and to such a part of the country, that he could not have been an immigrant; a comparison of the dates and places of residence has in several cases enabled the Committee to connect them to some family whose line has been carried further back one or more generations.

We propose, therefore, to suggest to the Association that the form for application to membership be a very simple one and that supplementary genealogical forms be devised, which will be sent only to those signifying their interest in such matters, and on which forms the family records can be so tabulated as to be used as clues in linking families together.

We have also to suggest the establishment of a Bureau of Genealogical Information, under an experienced genealogist, regularly engaged on behalf of the Association, to whom all members desiring information about their more remote ancestors, or desiring expert research in the Chamberlain line, can apply and have such work done at their individual expense,— the Association to have a copy of such results to go towards creating what may be called an Information Fund, which latter in time will be so complete and carefully arranged as to require only the labor of transcribing in order to answer almost every inquiry about any member's remote ancestors; in other words, expert research for Chamberlain ancestors will be centralized.

Our growing membership and a desire for genealogical records may show us that such a central bureau of information can not only be self-supporting but will permit of the classification of the genealogical information in such a way as to bring together a number of what appear to be distinct families of our name, and in this connection it may be interesting to say, that, among the six heads of families or branches heretofore mentioned, two, Henry and Richard, appear to be very closely related; and three, Thomas, William, and Edmund, are undoubtedly brothers; so we may expect to link together some of these branches and discover a common ancestor on the other side of the water, if not among the earliest immigrants.

Respectfully submitted,

THE GENEALOGICAL COMMITTEE,

J. C. CHAMBERLAIN,

Chairman.

A resolution was passed accepting the report of the Genealogical Committee and referring the suggestions contained therein to the Executive Committee.

The President very touchingly referred to the recent death of Dr. Cyrus N. Chamberlain, of Andover, Mass., the Chairman of the Executive Committee, and a committee was appointed to draft suitable resolutions in reference to the same. The committee subsequently reported the following, which was adopted by a rising vote :

"*Whereas*, It has pleased the Giver of life to remove from our sight a beloved and distinguished associate, Dr. Cyrus N. Chamberlain ; and

"*Whereas*, We desire to express our affectionate regard and our appreciation of his high character and eminent service : be it therefore

"*Resolved*, That this Association cherishes with tenderest regard and holds in highest honor the character and service of our departed companion, Dr. Cyrus N. Chamberlain ; we note also with pride his sterling personal qualities, his honorable career in private and professional life, and his eminent service to the country in the war for the Union. He has left us an inspiring example of what can be achieved of noble living, and we commend this to our successors.

"*Resolved*, That this resolution be spread upon the records of the Association, and that a copy of the same be sent to his family, with the assurance of our deepest sympathy."

LAURA B. CHAMBERLAIN,
MONTAGUE CHAMBERLAIN,
ASA W. CHAMBERLAIN,
Committee.

The Committee on English Ancestry, represented by the Chairman, Rev. L. T. Chamberlain, D. D., reported that some work had been done, principally in the way of correspondence and some outlay of means, and the outlook for this branch of the work is most encouraging.

The name of "Committee on Colonial and American Revolutionary Ancestry" was changed by vote to "Committee on Colonial and Revolutionary History."

The entire Board of Officers and Standing Committees of last year were reëlected for the ensuing year, with the exception that the Executive Committee was authorized to fill the vacancy upon that Committee caused by the death of Dr. Cyrus N. Chamberlain.

A meeting of the Executive Committee was held at the close of the meeting of the Association, at which action was taken looking to the establishment of a Genealogical Bureau, and the matter was placed in the hands of a committee consisting of Mr. Jacob Chester Chamberlain, Rev. L. T. Chamberlain, D. D., and Miss Jennie Chamberlain Watts. That committee at an adjourned meeting of the Executive made the following report :—

This special committee, after considering the suggestions in the report of the Genealogical Committee, at this morning's meeting, have to recommend the establishment of the proposed Genealogical Bureau, under the direction of that Committee, and that they engage a competent Bureau Secretary, who shall be an experienced genealogist ; this Bureau to collect and classify all Chamberlain records received from members, and practically carry on the genealogical correspondence.

It is proposed to issue a circular as soon as practicable, explaining the working plan of this Bureau, and giving the most interesting facts relating to the earliest immigrants or heads of families as outlined in the report referred to. Any members desiring information along lines of their own in the Chamberlain families may therefore have this work prosecuted through this Bureau to such an extent and at whatsoever expense they may specify, the charges or fees for such work to be according to rules hereafter determined upon by the Committee; these fees to form a fund which shall be disbursed by the Genealogical Committee in the prosecution of researches by competent persons engaged for this purpose. The researches and investigations will be made in the earliest town, state and church records, especially along such lines as will result in obtaining information and data of interest to the greatest number among our members, and which may be published in the Annual Reports, and ultimately in a volume comprising a Family History which we hope may be made a credit to this Association.

The funds for this work shall be derived, *first*, from such fees as may be received from members or other persons for information already obtained and in the possession of the Committee; *second*, from the appropriations which may be made from the funds of the Association by its authorized officers; *third*, from such donations as may be made toward such researches.

In this connection, this Committee have the pleasure to report that the Association is not now to be called upon for any appropriations, for a fund of $300 has been generously placed at the disposal of the Genealogical Committee to inaugurate and develop the Bureau plan, which we hope will not only maintain but greatly increase the interest in this Association.

Respectfully submitted,

J. C. CHAMBERLAIN,
L. T. CHAMBERLAIN,
JENNIE C. WATTS.

The Executive Committee by vote accepted the report of the special committee and empowered that committee to proceed with the organization of the Genealogical Bureau on the plan proposed.

LEANDER T. CHAMBERLAIN.

THE RECEPTION.

At three o'clock the company, augmented by many additional members and guests, assembled in the main drawing-room of the Parker House, where they were received by the President, General Joshua L. Chamberlain, assisted by General Samuel E. Chamberlain and Mrs. Chamberlain. Some two hours or more were spent in making acquaintances, which were facilitated by a corps of ushers, and in striving to unravel the mysteries of the family connection. Numbers of the clan were conspicuously proud of their ability to trace their line through generation after generation back to one of the earlier immigrants, while others were as conspicuously aware that they had no ancestors — they were nobody's great-grandchild.

This work of connecting the unattached with their proper branches is being pushed forward rapidly by the Genealogical Committee, and much interesting information is being gathered which will be published so soon as some tangles can be unravelled and a few loose ends united.

Yet while the topic of ancestry seemed to dominate the conversation, the prevailing sentiment was that social intercourse and fraternity and good fellowship made up the sum of the afternoon's enjoyment.

THE BANQUET.

After a recess, the company again assembled, this time in the "crystal" dining room, where, upon a fair white cloth, a goodly feast was spread.

Prayer was offered by the Rev. William Strong, and then the Chamberlain appreciation of the chef's skill was duly manifested.

Hunger being satisfied, with much flow of wit and humor and good fellowship to help on digestion, the company obeyed promptly the President's call to order, and settled themselves comfortably for the reception of the intellectual pabulum which was anticipated — and with which they were richly and generously served.

THE PRESIDENT.

We have much to congratulate ourselves upon at this time,— in fact that we have held this meeting! Amidst so many changes of date and confusions of convenience, we have actually held on to a date until you could all come to get it!

The trouble was that your Executive Committee, seeking for the most auspicious day for this meeting, found themselves tied fast by a By-Law,— and the Chamberlains are very obedient to the Laws,— fixing this on the second Wednesday in August.

This cut short all debate on their part; but it opened a very free one from those who received this notice. Much forensic talent was exhibited in this debate and much spirit in this "recessional"—from the 9th to the 16th, the 23d, and finally the 30th instant. I assure you it was no very pleasant thing for any of us to have to arrange adjournments and renew appointments as one and another unexpected obstacle had to be overcome. Now, however, you have this matter all fixed for the future, having "suspended the rules," and unanimously selected the "middle of September" as your crowning day.

I sought last year to entertain you with some pleasantries on the etymological origin of our name. From the tone of some of your letters this year, I expected to be asked to show the identity of elements in the first syllable of our name with chance and change. But I assure you there is not a syllable of truth in it. We are keepers, not changers, by name and by nature. Still let us not turn a cold shoulder upon those words. Change, from the strangely made up low Latin "*cambiare*," implies a certain facility in flank movements, in getting around obstacles we can't get over. Of this, certainly we have had some experience. And chance,—"*cadentia*,"— even if carrying some suggestion of instability, or even a tendency to tumble down,— yet stands for cheering proximity to the keynote — a pleasing cadence — a triumphant close. This, also, is well in evidence here. So we need not fear the alliterative charge, from the ranks of old French "*cha*."

There are changes, however, not of our ordering, before which we bow with supreme trust. Two whose words were among our brightest greetings at our last meeting, have been called to their place in other "sweet societies" to which they ever belong. President Bartlett's voice now swells the full symphony on high. Dr. Cyrus Chamberlain lives in other lives into which he has poured the richness of his own. We may greet him even as here.

> " Nor count me all to blame if I
> Conjecture of another guest
> Perchance, perchance, among the rest
> And though in silence, wishing joy."

I ask Miss Laura Chamberlain to read the resolutions adopted at our business session.

" *Whereas*, It has pleased the Giver of life to remove from our sight a beloved and distinguished associate, Dr. Cyrus N. Chamberlain ; and

" *Whereas*, We desire to express our affectionate regard and our appreciation of his high character and eminent service ; be it therefore

" *Resolved*, That this Association cherishes with tenderest regard and holds in highest honor the character and service of our departed companion, Dr. Cyrus N.

Chamberlain; we note also with pride his sterling personal qualities, his honorable career in private and professional life, and his eminent service to the country in the war for the Union. He has left us an inspiring example of what can be achieved of noble living, and we commend this to our successors.

"*Resolved*, That this resolution be spread upon the records of the Association, and that a copy of the same be sent to his family, with the assurance of our deepest sympathy."

God grant us all so sweet a remembrance!

We are happy in winning the favor of so distinguished an associate as our orator, to whom we will now give delighted attention. I present the Rev. Dr. Leander T. Chamberlain of New York.

Dr. Leander T. Chamberlain.

Mr. President and Members of the Association:

I thank you, Mr. President, for the very kind words in which you have introduced me, and you, kinsfolk, for the approval which you have so cordially expressed. It appeared to me that the invitation of this Association was not an ordinary invitation, even as the Association itself is not an ordinary Association. You remember that the visiting Englishman said to the American, "Then you have no House of Lords in this country?" "No," was the reply; "this is a nation without a peer." Similarly, we can say that this is an Association without a peer! And still it includes some very clever people. You know Dr. Holmes said, "The axis of the earth sticks out visibly through the center of each village."

And the introduction by our honored President reminds me of our first interview. I saw, at a glance, that he bore distinct resemblance to my own father who died many years ago; but to make sure that I might count myself his kinsman, I asked him if he knew anything about his great-grandfather; for, hitherto, no true Chamberlain has been supposed to know his forbears of even the third generation. Our President admitted that his genealogical lore did not, at that time, go back so far. And then he told me a characteristic anecdote of his grandfather Chamberlain, in whose possession were a presumably historic sword and gun. It appeared that our President, then a mere lad, eagerly asked his grandfather about those relics. A few brief facts were stated in reply, and then the old gentleman said impressively, "My son, it is of much more consequence how we comport ourselves in our own day than that we be informed about our ancestors."

With that typically Chamberlain sentiment I substantially agree. He was not far from right who said, "When a man talks mainly of his ancestors, you may know that the best part of his family is under ground." And yet, even if that does suggest the potato, probably there is no special merit in resembling the orchid, which is all branches and no roots. Moreover, almost anything may be put to some use. The dweller in the flat said to his friend, "The one trouble is that we are terribly cramped for space." "Is that so?" "Yes. We even have to use the family skeleton for a hat-rack." And enthusiastic Mrs. Newrich also had an eye to the utilities, when she confessed her great disappointment in not being able to get the shades of her ancestors for her parlor windows!

Yet nowadays the genealogical enthusiasm is spreading, even if an occasional Mrs. Kelley doesn't fully approve. They say Mrs. O'Brien asked her neighbor, Mrs. Kelley, if she had any ancestors. "And phwat are ancistors, Mrs. O'Brien?" "Why, people you've sphrung from." "Lishten to me, Mrs. O'Brien. Oi come from the stock of the Donahues, phwat sphrings from nobody; they sphrings *at* 'em." The genealogical enthusiasm, I say, is spreading, though there still are some who don't fully understand and appreciate. Said the young lady, "It was my good fortune that my ancestors came over in the Mayflower." "May flour!" exclaimed her friend. "Our folks made their fortune in September wheat!" And that, by the way, reminds me of the little girl who was asked who .

the Apostles were. "Oh," she answered, "they were those who followed the Saviour, and when He died they landed at Plymouth!" She doubtless was a New England girl, who had been taught the honor of descent from the heroes of 1620. And speaking thus of some who don't quite understand, I recall the lady who was showing a friend over her beautiful, spacious grounds. Said the friend, referring to a somewhat rare plant, "Doesn't this plant belong to the Bignonia family?" "To the Bignonia family!" was the excited answer. "Certainly not. It is ours, and always has been."

Doubtless there are those who are inclined to say concerning genealogy, as the pupil, in his geography lesson, wrote concerning the Arctic Ocean. He wrote, among other things, "The Arctic Ocean is used principally for purposes of exploration." And I dare say that the mark of a true genealogist is that he enjoys the pursuit itself, somewhat as philosophers enjoy the quest for truth, or as the born fisherman enjoys the art and the article of fishing. But for all that, there are likely to be various feelings roused, and some curious experiences encountered, in genealogical researches. It is usually understood, I believe, that the proper use of genealogy is to deepen reverence for those who have gone before, and to inspire a spirit of emulation such as Themistocles confessed, when he said, "The trophies of

Miltiades will not let me sleep." But it would be quite too much to expect that the effect should always be just that. It is more than possible that though we should confine our explorations to the family tree, we should still be led, now and then, to think we had caught glimpses of an arboreal ancestry, and to sympathize with the man who thoughtfully declared, "I am prepared to believe that there are those who are descended from monkeys; and that, in some cases, it has been considerable of a descent." He who looks up his progenitors is not unlikely, in some cases, to adopt the rendering which the Professor gave to the words *Requiescat in pace.* "Pa, what is the translation of *Requiescat in pace?*" "Well, my son, Please stay dead, is near enough." Probably the granddaughter was not sufficiently old to be a member of a genealogical association, at the time her grandmother put her to bed unusually early by way of corrective discipline. Yet it was presumed by those who knew the child, that she would make a remark or two, at the breakfast table the next morning, and they were not disappointed. In a pause in the general conversation, she quietly announced that she had dreamed of going to the place which is not Paradise. She said, "I knocked. Satan opened the door and asked, 'Who is it?' I answered, 'A naughty little girl.' 'Walk in,' he said, showing me into a very hot little room in which was a sofa covered with black hair-cloth. I sat down on the sofa, but Satan said, 'Get up instantly.' 'Why can't I sit on the sofa?' 'Because I am reserving that for your grandmother'!" And that granddaughter must have been akin to the boy who, looking at himself in the mirror, said to his father, "Father, did God make you?" "Yes." "Did he make me?" "Yes." "Well, God has been doing better work of late, hasn't He?" And that will do as an offset to an account which a friend gave me the other day, of a play once devised by the German Ambassador in Italy, who had been annoyed by the persistent attempts of his Italian acquaintances to make a German the butt of ridicule.

In the play to which the Ambassador lavishly invited his Italian friends, and the scene of which was laid in Rome, a man approaches a Roman café, very late at night. Striking a match, he looks at his watch, and says, "It is already past one o'clock; I don't much mind retiring; I think I will enter the café, and while away the time reading my Cicero." Thereupon the shade of Cicero, who is supposed to revisit Rome once in a thousand years, enters, and looking over the shoulder of the reader, says, "What wonderful handwriting!" "That is not writing, but printing from movable types." "Ah, that then is one of the great discoveries of the modern Romans." "No, it is a German invention." "But you drew the lightning from your pocket as you entered; that must be a Roman device!" "No, it is German." "But you looked at something in your hand and, in the absence of both sun and stars, you declared the time of day. That surely is a Roman contrivance!" "No; it, too, is German." "Well! If the wild German tribes whom I used to know have thus advanced, what must my own Romans be?" The man turned and, pointing to an Italian with a hand-organ and a monkey, said, "There is a sample."

And this leads us to the truth that the genealogical zeal which is at all worthy, is a zeal which keeps in effective relationship with the current life and, despite the fondness for dates and lineages, maintains a clear perception of merit and demerit, progress and decline.

In the founding of this Association I took a deep and serious interest, for the reason that it appeared worth while to do what promised not only to intensify the sense of kinship, but also greatly to broaden its horizon. I thought then, and I think now, that if it is natural and useful to cherish the bonds of the immediate family, it cannot be either foolish or futile to cherish the not dissimilar bonds which include remoter ancestors, and which relate even the outcomes of widely separated centuries and widely separated lands. This also is part of that *commune vinculum* which unites the race, and of that *amor humanitatis* which invests each member of the race with somewhat of affection and esteem.

That, Mr. President, is not an idle sentiment which makes us quick to note the mention of our line, and causes us to care whether the mention is with praise or blame. I submit that there is calculable value in whatever, so to speak, enlarges our personality; and that there is available power in whatever tends to centralize in us those good influences which are varied and remote. The merit of genealogical research is akin to that of other historical studies; and the almost unequaled excellence of historical study is in the fact that it not only acquaints us with the general lessons which the annals of events are fitted to teach, but also gives us, in effect, a part and place in the events themselves. I shall never forget the hour when "Plutarch's Lives" came into my boyish hands, and I read the stories of Theseus and Romulus, Lycurgus and Numa, Demosthenes and Cicero, Solon and Valerius Publicola; — catching thus some glimpse of "The beauty that was Greece, the grandeur that was Rome." It was almost as if I were partner in the founding of States and the making of laws; in the leading of armies and the subduing of kingdoms; in the pronouncing of the orator's discourse, and the framing of the sage's maxims. Accordingly, from that hour to this, I have pitied him who did

28

not enlarge and supplement the days and years of his own brief existence by living, more or less, in the times and the scenes to which history gives access and welcome. One's own lot may be never so humble, but if his converse, his companionship, is with the priests and prophets, the philosophers and princes, the poets and philanthropists, the adventurers and discoverers, the martyrs and saints, who already have lived and loved, he is favored and blest. In comparison with the citizen of to-day who grossly takes the modern material comforts, saying in act, if not in words, "Let us eat and drink, for to-morrow we die," one might be pardoned for admitting with Wordsworth,

" I'd rather be a pagan, suckled in a creed outworn,
So might I, standing on this pleasant lea,
Have glimpses that should make me less forlorn :
Have sight of Proteus rising from the sea,
Or hear old Triton blow his wreathèd horn."

It is a goodly thing to breathe the air which is truly circumambient, and to drink of the waters which, flowing ever seaward, yet take their rise among the cloud-capped heights. Meannesses and mendacities are plainly not in keeping with the measure of the ages and the march of the peoples.

It stands, then, that the true mission of an Association like this, is not to nourish pedantry or sanction petty pride. Its office is to remind us by the ties of an enlarged yet personal consanguinity, that God has made of one family all dwellers on the earth, and that, by the same infallible token, all are brethren. Its deep purpose is to render lucid and vivid to us the fact that,

> " There is no caste in blood
> Which runneth of one hue ; nor caste in tears
> Which trickle salt in all."

And I speak thus earnestly and frankly, because it is more than a theoretical danger which confronts us. Who has not seen, now and then, a superciliousness which fed its hollow pretensions on the fact that somewhere, at some time, somebody of the family name had attained to position and renown. A vacuous vanity, so ridiculous as to bring to mind the remark of the little girl who, walking with her mother, saw a typical dude. "Mamma, what is that?" "That, my child, is what they call a dude." "Did God make him?" "Yes." "Well, then, God likes to have fun sometimes, doesn't He?" Or the remark of the frontiersman who somewhere encountered a similar specimen,—"I say, Bill! What things a feller does see, when he hasn't his gun with him!"

I should like right well to know how many worthy men and women there are whose surnames, or whose descent, I share. And I should also like to know their dwelling-place, and by what paths life is leading them. Not, however, that I may embellish myself with their decorations, nor hide my own vulgarity under the tokens of their just distinctions. So far from that, I crave the knowledge, that I may be led to emulate their nobility, and to recognize my relationship with all the true and good.

The day of the tribe has gone by. The family abides, for the reason that the family is the unit and the germ. The family is the earthly fountain and source, *fons et origo*, of both institutions and laws. Therefore the duration of the family will be coeval with that of either Church or State. But the makeshift, the scaffolding, of tribal relations has already fallen away, with the coming of the grander ideal of the oneness of mankind. Similarly, distinctions national, and even racial, are more and more to be modified, as the true ideal prevails. The divinely ordered gravitation is toward a recovered unity, even as it is toward a regenerated life.

And I care to mention national distinctions as destined to be less and less forceful, in at least their restrictive, divisive sense and working, for the reason that I have in mind that imperfect, inconsistent patriotism with which, just now, many of our countrymen are so greatly enamoured. That faulty, though current patriotism, which practically asserts that love of one's native land sometimes necessitates the forgetting of moral distinctions, and may, on occasion, demand the setting aside of conscience' claims.

Be assured, however, that I am not proposing to mar the amenities of an occasion like this, by any discussion of "Expansion," or "Imperialism," or "Party Policy," nor yet of those "Wars of conquest" which President McKinley has emphatically characterized as *"criminal aggression."* I shall cast no slightest reproach on that love of country, which makes sacrifice and death, in the country's rightful service, sweet and glorious.

In my own day, I have carried the flag, and I have kept faithful step to the "music of the Union." I still say with Addison, "There is no greater sign of a general decay of virtue in a nation, than a want of zeal in its inhabitants for the good of their country." I aver with Shakespeare, "Had I a dozen sons, each in my love alike, and none less dear than thine and my good Marcius, I had rather had eleven die nobly for their country, than one voluptuously surfeit out of action."

Yet I am moved to mention national sentiment, national distinctions, as destined to be more and more modified, in at least their divisive sense and working, and distinctly to raise the issue here and now, for the three-fold reason, that this is an audience competent to judge; this a center where of old the equitable view prevailed; and that precisely here, at this heart of my native Commonwealth, there has been the recent, public announcement of the doctrine which, I think, deserves denial. Here, accordingly, let me speak certain words, as Heraclitus of Ephesus said of the words of the Sibyl, "solemn, unsweetened, unadorned."

I am told, it is on record, that the other day a vast Boston assembly boisterously cheered the catchword, "My country, right or wrong," as it fell from the lips of a distinguished soldier; and I recently had in my hand the printed, lauded statement of Boston's "First Citizen," to wit, "I hold it to be the duty of the citizens of any nation to support the government as against other nations, and to trust in the authorities of the country, to whom is confided the administration of the nation's affairs."

Still observe, I pray you, that my protest is on grounds moral, ethical, universal. And therein, permit me to say, I am encouraged and supported by the word of Abraham Lincoln, "Let us have faith that right makes might, and in that faith let us dare to do our duty as we understand it."

In the light, then, of ethical principle, how insensate is the statement, "My country, right or wrong!" A statement which, in its very terms, destroys the moral basis of both Society and the State, and stupidly mocks the righteous government of God. I can conceive a madness which should say, "Whatever my country does, *is* right"; but certainly it is not easy to appreciate the intellectual as well as moral idiocy which shouts, "My country, right or *wrong*." As well announce that God is God, except as He fails to sanction my country's course; or to aver that right is right, save as it opposes my country's desire. It is, in terms, declaring that the first commandment is not, "Thou shalt love the Lord with all thy heart," but "Thou shalt do as thy government bids." It is, in terms, proclaiming that the second commandment is not, "Thou shalt love thy neighbor as thyself," but "Thou shalt follow the flag." It would seem that that palpable, silly blasphemy might, at last, be permitted to become obsolete.

And how better is the statement, "I hold it to be the duty of the citizens of any nation to support the government as against other nations"? That unqualified statement fairly means, although I can hardly believe that its distinguished author had fully in mind its evil purport, that the cause of one's own nation is to dominate the cause of any and every opposing nation. It means that it is the duty of each good citizen to uphold his country's wars, though they be wars of cruelty and oppression. It means that all subjects whose ruler is Philip II, and the majority of whose fellow subjects are Philip's supporters, should heartily lend their aid in crushing the Free Netherlands; that all faithful Russians, Prussians, and Austrians should support their governments in the dismembering of Poland; and, by inference, that all Turks should help the Sultan in slaughtering the uneasy Armenians. It means that the prophets were unworthy citizens in their foretelling, with approval, of the deserved captivities of their own Israel; and that our Saviour himself was unpatriotic in publicly predicting the deserved breaking down of the Jewish national rule. It means that Burke and Pitt and Fox, in their support of our claims of independence, were renegade Englishmen; and that our Quakers are, to this day, guilty apostates from the true civic faith. Assuredly that doctrine is false and foul, and the statement that bears such an import, deserves condemnation.

I sincerely trust that wherever a Chamberlain is found, in either name or blood, there there will be found one who, in theory at least, loves God supremely; and one who believes, without reservation, that the highest welfare of the great brotherhood of man is to be regarded as at least equal to the temporary victory of his own possibly wilful or mistaken country. Certainly I, for one, shall continue to think that we have fallen on evil times, when right is controllingly conditioned by earthly

35

affiances, and when the path of personal honor is dictated by the trend of national, political preference.

In other words, I trust that wherever this Association has a member, there there will be a patriot who stands, in all things, for what is righteous and genuine and useful.

And saying that, let me also hasten to say that I am not, as you are not, averse to the gracious, the beautiful, the freely joyous. It takes nothing from the strength of the pillars, that lily-work encircles them, or that their capitals are carved with acanthus leaf and involute scroll. I confess that, as against the mad haste which strides through beds of flowers as through bog and fen, and as against the wasteful utility which demands that everything shall be reckoned by tables of profit and loss, I have a veritable sympathy with the story of the brook,—

"The little shallow brook that ran
Between low banks scarcely a child's leap wide,
Feeding a foot or two of bordering grass
And, here and there, some tufts of water-flowers
And cresses, tall sedge, rushes, and reeds.
And where it bubbled past a poor man's cot,
He and his household came and drank of it,
And all the children loved it for its flowers,
And counted it a playmate made for them.
But, not far off, a sandy arid waste
Where, when a winged seed rested, or a bird

Would drop a grain in passing. and it grew,
It presently must droop and die athirst,—
Spread its scorched, silent leagues to the fierce sun.
And once a learned man came by and saw,
And " Lo," said he, "what space for corn to grow,
Could we send vivifying moistures here ;
While, see, this wanton, misdirected brook
Watering its useless weeds."   So had it turned,
And made a channel for it through the waste.
But its small waters could not feed that drought,
And in the wide, unshadowed plain, it lagged
And shrunk away, sucked upwards of the sun
And downwards of the sands.   So the new bed
Lay dry, and dry the old.   And the parched reeds
Grew brown and dwined ; the stunted rushes drooped ;
The cresses could not root in that slack soil ;
The blossoms and the sedges died away ;
The greenness shriveled from the dusty banks ;
The children missed their playmate and the flowers,
And thirsted in hot noon-tides for the draught
Grown over-precious, now the mother went
A half mile to the well to fill her pail.
And not an ear of corn the more was green !"

Good friends, the stress, the rush, which gives no
space for mirth and music, and has no use for smiles
and laughter, is not the gift of God.   It is the device
of foolish, sinful men.

At the same time, there is a work to be done ;
for the sad world is to be comforted, the suffering
world is to be relieved, the sinning world is to be

37

set right. That means both prayer and toil, and it puts one in the mood of Mrs. Browning, in "Aurora Leigh,"

> "Who has time,
> An hour's time,— think — to sit upon a bank
> And hear the cymbals tinkle in white hands?
> When Egypt's slain, I say, let Miriam sing.
> Before,— where's Moses."

It calls to mind the words of gifted, grand old William Blake,

> "Bring me my bow of burning gold,
> Bring me my arrows of desire,
> Bring me my spear. O clouds, unfold.
> Bring me my chariot of fire.

> "I will not cease from mental fight,
> Nor shall my sword sleep in my hand,
> Till we have built Jerusalem
> In all this green and pleasant land."

It thus comes home to us that, under the inspirations of this fellowship, within the bonds of this alliance, we are to consecrate ourselves to the genuine and the useful, along with the beautiful and the pure. We are to bear in mind the word of Goethe,

> "Like the star that shines afar,
> Without haste and without rest,
> Let each man wheel with steady sway
> Round the task that rules the day,
> And do his best."

Success, then, to the Chamberlain Association. Let its plans be perfected, its efforts redoubled, its progress be put on helpful record. Let it be devotedly cherished by each member, and let its membership be constantly enlarged. Let us take as our motto the words of George Eliot, "It is ever to be borne in mind that the end of all learning, of all science, of all life in fact, is that human beings should love one another better."

Then shall we, in our organized relation, be a worthy part of the still larger fellowship, even of the universal brotherhood. One good deed will incite to another, one worthy thought will inspire a second, one noble life will encourage its still nobler counterpart, and the federation will be immortal. For it is the wondrous privilege of the children of light that their elect kindred are to be found everywhere and in all periods of time.

"Ah, strange the bond that in one great life binds
All master-moments of all master-minds!
Strange the one clan that years nor wars destroy,
The undispersed co-heritage of joy!
Strange that howe'er the sounding ages roll,
From age to age shall soul encounter soul,
Across the dying times, the world's dim roar,
Speak each with each and live forevermore!
So have I seen in some deep wood divine,
The dark and silvery stems of birch and pine;
Apart they sprang, rough ground between them lay

Tangled with brambles and with briars, but they
Met at their summits, and the rushing breeze
Inlocked the topmost murmur of the trees."

THE PRESIDENT.

Now we turn to the church militant. It was one
of the honors of my life to have assigned to my command in 1864 the Brigade made up of regiments
like the splendid 150th Pennsylvania, which on the
first immortal day at Gettysburg had snatched gar-
lands of glory from the gates of death. I now greet
here, that companion of heroic days, then a field
officer of that Regiment,— since, its commander,—
Colonel Thomas Chamberlin of Philadelphia.

COLONEL THOMAS CHAMBERLIN.

With no anticipation of a call to speak, I fail to
have a "neat little impromptu" stored in the re-
cesses of my memory, duly seasoned for this occasion.

Indeed, in coming to Boston, my object was to
keep eyes and ears alert for any good thing in the
air, leaving to others the agreeable task of talking.
It seemed highly improbable that anybody would
care to hear from one living near the confines of
Berks County, Penn'a,— that delectable region
where Andrew Jackson continues to be the standing

candidate for the presidency; and as to entering the lists for a friendly tilt of words with people whose daily fare is supposed to be "salt cod," and plenty of it,— the thought never occurred to me. The mind of the Pennsylvanian works slowly in some directions. It has a keen appreciation of a joke — when it catches the "point" of it; but the absorption and enjoyment of a bit of humor is often so belated that the attendant "guffaw" creates a doubt of the laugher's sanity. In our endless struggle with material things, we are apt to neglect the development of our higher mental powers, from which it results that New England outshines us, possibly, in pulpit and forum, and Pennsylvania is to-day without a representative in the national Congress capable of saying the fitting word, in a fitting way, for the second most populous and important State of the Union.

In matters political we follow the lead of the " Boss," and of that particular " Boss " who shakes the largest and most luscious " plums " into our lap. But make no mistake about it. *We are too busy to have time for politics.* Our energies are employed in extracting from the earth the mineral wealth with which a generous Providence has stuffed our hills and valleys, and from this our State has grown rich and populous and muscular, with ample store of patriotism, and such resources of fighting material for our army and navy as would have driven our Quaker founder to a premature grave.

But my thoughts are apparently out for a holiday, and must be brought to order. Permit me to say that I regard it as a very great honor to have been named as one of the Vice-Presidents of this Association, whose work, already fairly begun, promises to be both interesting and important. Before the stone was quarried for its foundation, in a correspondence with people of our name in various parts of the West, I was made aware that a goodly portion of the family was gifted with bright mentality, which flashed like electric light through all its letters. Whether this is a happy inheritance from an ancestry of superior intelligence, or the result of a discovery of fish-ball mines in the Western States, by which the New England monopoly of brain food has been broken, is a problem whose solution is left to others. Suffice it to say that wherever Chamberlains are found we need not be ashamed of their mental endowment.

At the time of the Revolution our particular branch was a little less numerous in the northern counties of New Jersey than the locusts of Egypt, but it formed a productive, not a destructive, class, being mostly hard-working farmers. The name was Chamber*lain*, as shown by the archives of New Jersey, and confirmed by the recollections of their numerous descendants. My grandfather shared the common ambition of the family — to be the owner of a grist-mill,— and held such a piece of realty in Amwell Township, Hunterdon County. Being in need of a branding-iron with which to mark his flour-barrels, he had one made by a neighboring black-smith, who, by some oversight, allowed the "a" to drop out in forging the final syllable of the name. A pardonable piece of "forgery," my grandfather seemed to think ; for with flour on hand ready for the market, he chose not to wait for a new brand to be made, or the defective one corrected, but accepted the "botched job," and from that day — about 1770 — his barrels, billheads and books bore the name "William Chamber*lin*." His many successors (for the virile old colonel was married four times and had twenty-three children!) are, therefore, fully entitled to the additional "a," if disposed to adopt it ; but regarding the manner of spelling the name as largely a matter of individual fancy, they are content to spell it with as little waste to the alphabet as possible.

While heartily endorsing the social feature of our organization, I trust the main purpose of its forma-tion will be kept constantly in view, which is — I take it — to trace back the various family lines as far as possible towards their English or Continental sources, and ascertain what relationships, however remote, exist between our several American branches. When this is done, the Genealogical Committee can gather the results into a book, which, when published, will be the crowning work of our Association.

THE PRESIDENT.

It is said there was war in Heaven,— Michael the Archangel fighting the great dragon. We have with us one who fought the dragon—not exactly in Heaven,— in fact quite far from it. We have the Massachusetts *man* called to be South Carolina's Governor in the grave crisis of the Country's restoration, whose heroic effort to establish honor, truth, and the rights of manhood in the administration of human affairs, will ever brighten the pages of his country's history, and do honor to his name and ours. Here stands before you the Hon. Daniel H. Chamberlain, one of the most brilliant of men — the best farmer of Massachusetts!

HON. DANIEL H. CHAMBERLAIN.

Mr. President and Brethren of the Chamberlain Association:

Our President's words of introduction embarrass me. I am sure they are undeserved; but I cannot help thanking him for uttering them and you all for receiving them so cordially.

Our President needs no eulogium from any of us. The world knows and honors him. Scholar, soldier, statesman, he has filled out a career of varied service to his generation such as few other men have achieved; and it may be added that but for the ill conditions of political advancement in his own State, he would still be in active public life, adding constantly new lustre to his own fame and fresh honor to the Chamberlain name. I can assure him that one of the chief pleasures I anticipated in attending this meeting was that of meeting him.

But I am not here for purposes of eulogy, however well deserved. I am here because I deem it a privilege as well as a duty to be here; for our object is to promote our knowledge of our ancestry and of those who now represent our name. It is becoming more and more clear to all minds, that men and women are largely, very largely, what their ancestry has made them. The mould of our being, the type of our character, the current of our life, has been fixed almost beyond change by the character, the moral and spiritual lineaments, of those from whom we have sprung. In thinking of this I am often reminded of the words of our most brilliant American historian : " The present and the future are clay in the hands of the past." This is true of nations and of individuals, of races and of families. But it is especially true of us all in respect to our family relations. If we are distinguished by our race, and by our nation, much more are we marked by our family, by the immediate line of family descent through which we come. The greatest of all modern words is evolution. It denotes the universal law of development. We spring from the past. We come dowered with a good ancestry, or burdened by a poor. But be it good or poor, we cannot escape its influence. We may largely overcome or increase ancestral tendencies but none of us can escape them, struggle as we may. Our life comes to us charged with influences which run back far into the past. The type of character is stronger, more ineffaceable, than the type of feature. Moral likeness is more certain to appear from generation to generation than physical likeness.

The ancestral influences are to some extent irregular. They certainly are, as Galton has expressed it, saltatory. They leap; they pass over generations; but they are persistent. They re-appear in all their vigor in due time.

Well, if we do come charged and fashioned by a past, by a long and unbroken line of influences which make us what we essentially are, then who can hesitate to feel that it is wise to study those influences, to study them in the lives, the history, the character of our strict family ancestors? We are all Chamberlains. We cannot change that fact, if we would;

we are Chamberlains not in name merely, but inevitably in character. Differences of environment, of experience, of location, have distinguished us from each other; but who doubts that there is a Chamberlain type? Into that type enter many influences, some good, some doubtless not so good, some probably bad. But if we would do what we can to promote the good, to reform the less good, and to root out the bad, we must know our ancestral influences deeply and thoroughly.

Here to me lies the value of our association. Not over fond, by nature or inclination, of genealogical studies, I know the value to me of familiarity with my family ancestors. If there be traits I would cultivate, I must know them. If there be traits I would repress, I must know them. It was not of my own volition I came into this life. I came by the will of others. I came stamped with an image and a superscription,— the image of my ancestors, the superscription of Chamberlain. The image of my ancestors I must carry in my face and form, in my character and spirit. If I would elevate my family, if I would work together with all good ancestral influences, I must realize who the Chamberlains have been, what they have been, how they have met life, where they have succeeded, where they have failed; for it is of the essence of evolution that good tendencies may be cultivated, and bad tendencies may be repressed.

Great public questions have been discussed here to-night. With the sentiments expressed I am in full sympathy; but I shall not say more on those topics. To our country we owe our best services at all times, and at some times even our lives. We who were in our youth or prime thirty-five years ago can never forget or cease to glory in the great days we then saw, the great dangers we then faced, and the great triumphs we then beheld. Glorious memories! Fadeless recollections! But the days crowd upon each other. New occasions bring new work. I can hardly conceive of a situation in which I could feel it to be my duty to refuse to support my country. Certainly the crisis must be one so clear, so strenuous, so commanding, that the path of duty cannot be mistaken.

But I come back to the thought which most deeply interests me now,—the thought of the influences, the weal or the woe, which are surely descending upon us all from the whole long line of those who have borne our name and have made us what we are. Into the study of those influences, I feel inspired by this meeting to enter more deeply and more ardently than ever before. I desire to cherish and cultivate a well-founded family pride. I deem it one of the chief supports of life to be able to turn with pride to one's ancestors, to fortify one's own failing resolutions by reverting to the heroism or self-sacrifice

48

of those whose blood flows in our veins, whose name we bear, and whose virtues and honors we would illustrate and advance by our own lives.

THE PRESIDENT.

When the Lord chose Joshua to deliver his people out of Egyptian bondage he commanded him to be strong. It would have been of no use so to command a weak man. He had first made him strong; he chose him because he was strong: he commanded him because he could be. One of that name and nature is of us,— still leading people out of darkness to light. We know him well: the Rev. Dr. E. E. Strong of Boston, editor of the "Missionary Herald."

Dr. Strong congratulated the Association upon its satisfactory and encouraging condition and rejoiced that he was connected with such a flourishing and brilliant family.

THE PRESIDENT.

Last year I proved to you how much obliged to me our genial friend here, Mrs. General Samuel Chamberlain, was for my being the man who took on himself that mortal wound reported to have been received by her brave husband. Now I want to show you that I had good reason for it. He had had his share, and you will see which way he was fac-

ing when he took it,— the Colonel of your splendid First Massachusetts Cavalry, General Samuel
Chamberlain!

General Chamberlain said he was a man of action
rather than of words, but he must take friendly
issue with the orator of the evening. It is, he considered, the duty of every loyal citizen to support
the Government when that Government, acting on
the best information obtainable, determines upon a
policy which it believes is for the best interest of
the country.

THE PRESIDENT.

Leander swam the Hellespont merely to get near
a Hero. Our Leander swam all the oceans for four
years in our great war to find himself a hero. Your
hearts still vibrate under his massive eloquence. I
now present Leander T. Chamberlain, an officer of
the United States Navy.

Dr. Chamberlain told the story of his being
offered a position in the navy on leaving college,
and of his four years of service.

THE PRESIDENT.

I do not wish to waken vain regrets, nor stir up
bitter jealousies in the hearts of you men here; but

there is a girl among you who can beat you to death whistling! Your whistling is a mere reflex action of the nervous system when you are passing a grave-yard at midnight, or when you are at a loss what to do next : but this girl commands the music of the spheres. She knows how to turn the palpitations of the air into palpitations of your hearts,— Miss Ella Chamberlain!

Miss Chamberlain entertained the company with several pieces of delightful music rendered in her inimitable way.

THE PRESIDENT.

I recall the story of an excellent gentleman who was a guest at a festive occasion like this, and with wise forethought desiring to reinforce his powers of judgment in a possible future crisis, pinned his card of address in the inside of his hat. Some wag in the course of the evening, observant of present tenden-cies, removed this label to a hat of much smaller dimensions. Our hero among departing guests, rely-ing chiefly at that time on his written signature, took up a hat which bore this token, but still did not alto-gether suit him. When he tried it on, he himself was much tried, wondering how he had become so consid-erable an expansionist ; but he was disposed to be a little lenient towards his general consciousness, rely-ing solidly on his sober written declaration. He called a friend. "Will you tell me what the name is, in this hat?"—"Why, yes, it is William Smith."—"Well, then, that's my hat!" Acting vigorously in this belief he found the discrepancy certainly no less, and turning desperately to the by-stander, he exclaimed, "Now, sir, will you please to tell me who I be?" We have a psychical genius here, who can do that for us, under all circumstances. Even when we don't know ourselves, he can tell us who we are,— Mr. Jacob Chester Chamberlain of the Genealogical Committee.

Mr. Chamberlain read portions from the reports of the committees having charge of the genealogical work.

THE PRESIDENT.

Not long ago I received from the author a very remarkable little book modestly entitled "*Maliseet Vocabulary.*" This book not only showed long, patient industry in collecting words, but reached back to the laws of thought — the way in which things and their relations appear in a primitive condition of the human mind. It is a result also of a generous interest on the part of its author in a noble race of men whom we have displaced on these New England shores. You will be glad of one more word from Mr. Montague Chamberlain.

MR. MONTAGUE CHAMBERLAIN.

Mr. President and Colleagues:

I must thank the President for his kind words of introduction and for the complimentary terms in which he has referred to my little book; but it must seem to you like a far cry from the clan Chamberlain to the Indians; though perhaps if I tell you that my grandfather, Theophilus Chamberlain, was adopted as a son by a Penobscot brave who captured him during the fight at Ticonderoga, you may find more connection between the Chamberlains and the Indians than is apparent on the surface.

I will accept the opportunity to say a word in behalf of my Indian friends who have been much maligned by our writers. The older historians made monstrous blunders when writing about these Wapanaki tribes,—the circumstances under which they gathered their data rendered accuracy impossible,—and the more recent writers have followed their accounts, blunders and all. The nobility of the Indian life, before that life was disturbed by the European invasion,— their chivalry, their high sense of honor, their courtesy and kind consideration of others, the high moral plane upon which their plan of life was laid, the strictness with which they followed such religious light as had been granted to them, their downright honesty, their clean, healthy manliness — of these things the early New Eng-

53

landers knew little or nothing. Study their traditions and at the same time study the remnant of the people who are yet with us, and you will, I am sure, support my conclusion, that the Indians of those early days lived better lives — better according to the highest standard — than did the mass of the Puritans by whom they were maligned.

Miss Bertha Chamberlain, of Medfield, Mass., then played some selections on the piano, and short addresses were delivered by Mrs. Smiley, of Marblehead, Mass., and Mrs. Capron, of Winchendon, Mass.

Following these, by a standing vote, the company sent a message of kind sympathy and of cheer to the wife of the President, who was prevented by illness from being present.

A vote was also passed expressing fraternal good will for the Association of the Pennsylvania branch of the family, which met on September 8th.

The hour being late, the meeting adjourned.

TREASURER'S REPORT.

MRS. SOPHIA A. CASWELL, IN ACCOUNT WITH THE
CHAMBERLAIN ASSOCIATION.

1898.	DR.		
Sept. 1.	Balance on hand, . .		$58.30
	Membership fees,	$38.00	
	Life Member, . .	25.00	
	Subscriptions, .	100.00	
	Sale of Reports, . .	1.75	
	Postage paid, . .	.10	164.85
			$223.15

	CR.		
Sept. 22.	Printing, . . .	$4.85	
Oct. 18.	Paid Treasurer, . .	25.00	
Dec. 10.	Deficit of Banquet Account,	10.00	
Dec. 15.	Envelopes, . . .	1.00	
Jan. 2.	Printing By-Laws . .	17.00	
Aug. 7.	Printing Reports, . .	27.50	
Aug. 16.	Printing Invitations, .	4.50	
	Postage, post cards, .	11.85	
	Secretary for postage, etc.	4.79	
	Record Book . .	.75	$107.24
	Balance in hands of Asst. Treasurer,		$115.91
	In Treasurer's hands, . . .		25.00
	Total balance, . . .		$140.91

55

OFFICERS FOR THE CURRENT YEAR.

President.
MAJ.-GEN. JOSHUA L. CHAMBERLAIN, LL. D., Brunswick, Me.

Vice-Presidents.
HON. MELLEN CHAMBERLAIN, LL. D., Chelsea, Mass.
HON. DANIEL H. CHAMBERLAIN, LL. D., West Brookfield, Mass.
MAJOR-GEN. SAMUEL E. CHAMBERLAIN, Barre, Mass.
COL. THOMAS CHAMBERLIN, Philadelphia, Pa.
REV. E. E. STRONG, D. D., Boston, Mass.
PROF. T. C. CHAMBERLIN, LL. D., Chicago, Ill.
MYRON L. CHAMBERLAIN, M. D., Boston, Mass.
COL. SIMON E. CHAMBERLIN, Washington, D. C.

Corresponding Secretary.
MISS ABBIE M. CHAMBERLAIN, January to May, inclusive,
Washington, D. C.; June to December, inclusive, Box 218, Braintree, Mass.

Recording Secretary.
MR. ASA W. CHAMBERLIN, Jamaica Plain, Mass.

Treasurer.
MR. THOMAS CHAMBERLAIN, State National Bank, Boston.

Assistant Treasurer.
MRS. SOPHIA CHAMBERLAIN CASWELL, 27 River Street,
Cambridgeport, Mass.

Additional Members of Executive Committee.
MISS LAURA B. CHAMBERLAIN, Cambridge, Mass.
MR. MONTAGUE CHAMBERLAIN, Cambridge, Mass.

STANDING COMMITTEES.

Genealogical Committee.

MR. JACOB CHESTER CHAMBERLAIN, *Chairman*, 1 W. 81st Street, New York.

COL. THOMAS CHAMBERLIN, Philadelphia, Pa.

MR. HERBERT B. CHAMBERLAIN, Brattleboro, Vt.

J. W. CHAMBERLIN, M. D., St. Paul, Minn.

MISS JENNIE CHAMBERLAIN WATTS, Madison, Wis.

JOSEPH E. N. CHAMBERLAIN, M. D., Easton, Md.

Committee on Colonial and American Revolutionary History.

J. W. CHAMBERLIN, M. D., *Chairman*, Endicott Building, St. Paul, Minn.

MR. WILLIAM S. BOYNTON, St. Johnsbury, Vt.

MRS. H. H. BURNHAM, Putnam, Conn.

MRS. HELEN GUILFORD, Minneapolis, Minn.

MRS. O. A. FURST, Bellefonte, Pa.

MISS S. EMMA CHAMBERLIN, Cleveland, O.

MR. PRESCOTT CHAMBERLAIN, Boston, Mass.

Committee on English Ancestry.

REV. L. T. CHAMBERLAIN, D. D., *Chairman*, The Chelsea, New York.

REV. N. H. CHAMBERLAYNE, Monument Beach, Mass.

MRS. HARRIET P. KIMBALL, Dubuque, Iowa.

REV. JAMES A. CHAMBERLIN, Newark, N. J.

MR. HENRY R. CHAMBERLAIN, London, England.

LIST OF MEMBERS.

August 30, 1899.

(Those in heavy-faced type are "charter" members; those marked with an asterisk are dead.)

ACTIVE MEMBERS.

Col. H. H. ADAMS,	New York, N. Y.
Capt. A. P. ANDREW,	La Porte, Ind.
Mrs. MARTHA E. AUSTIN,	Roxbury, Mass.
Mrs. E. S. BARTLETT,	Evanston, Ill.
Mrs. Ellen E. C. Blair,	Dorchester, Mass.
Mr. D. C. BLOOMER,	Council Bluffs, Iowa.
Mrs. S. M. BODWELL,	Clifton Springs, N. Y.
Mr. William S. Boynton,	St. Johnsbury, Vt.
Mrs. J. M. Brant,	East Weymouth, Mass.
Mrs. GEORGE M. BROWN,	Hartford, Conn.
Mrs. J. S. BROWNE,	La Grange, Ind.
Mrs. Mary C. Burnham,	Putnam, Conn.
Mrs. CARRIE M. BUTTS,	Newton Centre, Mass.
Mrs. EMILY A. CAPRON,	Winchendon, Mass.
Mrs. Sophia A. C. Caswell,	Cambridgeport, Mass.
Miss Abbie M. Chamberlain,	Washington, D. C.
Mr. A. C. Allen Chamberlain,	Winchester, Mass.
Miss ALICE CHAMBERLAIN,	Hyde Park, Mass.
ALLEN H. CHAMBERLAIN, M. D.,	Foxcroft, Me.
Mr. ANSEL E. CHAMBERLIN,	Dalton, Mass.

58

Mr. **Asa W. Chamberlin,**	Jamaica Plain, Mass.
Mr. Burr C. Chamberlin,	Dalton, Mass.
Mr. Charles A. Chamberlin,	Westford, Mass.
Mr. Charles E. Chamberlin,	Roxbury, Mass.
Mr. Charles H. Chamberlin,	Dalton, Mass.
*Mr. Charles K. Chamberlin,	Pittsburg, Pa.
(Died May 14, 1899.)	
***Cyrus N. Chamberlain, M. D.,**	Andover, Mass.
(Died July 18, 1899.)	
Mr. Charles W. Chamberlain,	Dayton, Ohio.
Mr. C. W. Chamberlain,	Boston, Mass.
Hon. **Daniel H. Chamberlain, LL. D.,**	
	West Brookfield, Mass.
*Hon. **Daniel U. Chamberlin,**	Cambridgeport, Mass.
(Died June 15, 1898.)	
Mr. Dwight S. Chamberlain,	Lyons, N. Y.
Mr. **Edward Watts Chamberlain,**	Louisville, Ky.
Mr. Edwin A. Chamberlin,	Trenton, N. J.
Miss Elisabeth Chamberlin,	Torresdale, Pa.
Miss Elisabeth E. Chamberlain,	Providence, R. I.
Miss **Ella J. Chamberlain,**	Cambridge, Mass.
Mr. Elvord G. Chamberlain,	Montclair, N. J.
Mr. Ephraim Chamberlain,	Medfield. Mass.
Mr. Eugene C. Chamberlin,	Chicago, Ill.
Mr. Eugene Tyler Chamberlain,	Washington, D. C.
Gen. Frank Chamberlain,	Albany, N. Y.
Mr. Fred W. Chamberlin,	Detroit, Mich.
Mr. F. W. Chamberlain,	Three Oaks, Mich.
Mr. George R. Chamberlain,	New Haven, Conn.
Mr. **George W. Chamberlain,**	Weymouth, Mass.
Miss Gertrude Chamberlin,	Boston, Mass.

59

Miss Helen Chamberlain,	Hyde Park, Mass.
Mr. Henry R. Chamberlain,	London, England.
Mr. Herbert B. Chamberlin,	Brattleboro, Vt.
Mr. I. C. Chamberlain,	Dubuque, Iowa.
Miss Isabella S. Chamberlin,	Washington, D. C.
Rev. Jacob Chamberlain, D. D.	Madanapalle, India.
Mr. Jacob Chester Chamberlain,	New York, N. Y.
Rev. James A. Chamberlin,	Torrington, Conn.
Mr. James Roswell Chamberlin,	Rochester, N. Y.
Miss Jessie C. Chamberlin,	Boston, Mass.
Mr. John C. Chamberlin,	Dalton, Mass.
Joseph E. N. Chamberlain, M. D.,	Easton, Md.
Maj.-Gen. Joshua L. Chamberlain, LL. D.,	
	Brunswick, Me.
Mr. J. D. Chamberlin,	Toledo, Ohio.
J. P. Chamberlin, M. D.,	Boston, Mass.
J. W. Chamberlin, M. D.,	St. Paul, Minn.
Miss Laura B. Chamberlain,	Cambridge, Mass.
Miss Lizzie F. Chamberlain,	Cambridge, Mass.
Mr. Martin H. Chamberlin,	Rutland, Vt.
Miss Mary Chamberlin,	Torresdale, Pa.
McKendree H. Chamberlin, LL. D.,	Lebanon, Ill.
Hon. Mellen Chamberlain, LL. D.,	Chelsea, Mass.
Mr. Montague Chamberlain,	Cambridge, Mass.
Myron L. Chamberlain, M. D.,	Boston, Mass.
Mr. Newell Chamberlain,	Cambridge, Mass.
Miss N. A. Chamberlain,	Auburndale, Mass.
Rev. N. H. Chamberlayne,	Monument Beach, Mass.
Capt. Orville T. Chamberlain,	Elkhart, Ind.
Mr. Prescott Chamberlain,	Chelsea, Mass.

Miss PHŒBANNA CHAMBERLAIN,	Orange, N. J.
Gen. ROBERT H. CHAMBERLAIN,	Worcester, Mass.
Mr. ROLLIN S. CHAMBERLAIN,	Wilkesbarre, Pa.
Brig.-Gen. Samuel E. Chamberlain,	
	Barre Plain, Mass.
Miss Sarah P. Chamberlain,	Salem, Mass.
Col. Simon E. Chamberlin,	Washington, D. C.
Miss S. Emma Chamberlin,	Cleveland, Ohio.
Mr. S. T. CHAMBERLIN,	Derby, Conn.
Prof. T. C. Chamberlin, LL. D.,	Chicago, Ill.
Col. Thomas Chamberlin,	Philadelphia, Pa.
Mr. Thomas Chamberlain,	Hyde Park, Mass.
Mr. THOMAS E. CHAMBERLIN,	Brookline, Mass.
Mr. WILLARD N. CHAMBERLAIN,	Watertown, Mass.
Prof. WILLIAM B. CHAMBERLAIN,	Oak Park, Ill.
Mr. WILLIAM B. CHAMBERLIN,	Torresdale, Pa.
Mr. William Carlton Chamberlain,	Louisville, Ky.
Mr. WILLIAM JOSEPH CHAMBERLAIN,	Denver, Col.
Major WILLIAM N. CHAMBERLIN,	Washington, D. C.
Mr. WILLIAM PORTER CHAMBERLAIN,	Knoxville, Tenn.
Mr. WILLIAM S. CHAMBERLAIN,	Cleveland, Ohio.
Mrs. T. EATON CLAPP,	Albany, N. Y.
*****Mrs. Alice Gertrude C. Clarke,**	Southbridge, Mass.
(Died July 8, 1899.)	
Mrs. MARY L. C. CLARKE,	Andover, Mass.
Edward Cowles, M. D.,	Waverley, Mass.
Mrs. CORYDON CRAIN,	Jamaica Plain, Mass.
Mrs. T. W. DALE,	Auburndale, Mass.
Mrs. AMIE WHITING DAMON,	Reading, Mass.
Mrs. A. E. DICK,	Andover, Mass.
Mrs. KATE C. DILLINGHAM,	Denver, Col.

61

Mr. HARRIOTT A. FOX,	Chicago, Ill.
Mrs. Caroline W. Furst,	Bellefonte, Pa.
Miss M. E. GROVER,	White River Junction, Vt.
Mrs. Helen Guilford,	Minneapolis, Minn.
Mrs. O. H. HARDING,	Allston, Mass.
Miss Louise H. Hinckley,	Cambridge, Mass.
Miss LIDA HOOPER,	New York City, N. Y.
Mrs. H. T. C. HUGHES,	Mobile, Ala.
Mrs. CLEORA E. JEFFERDS,	Foxcroft, Me.
Miss CHARLOTTE A. JEWELL,	Hartford, Conn.
Mrs. ANNIE B. CHAMBERLAIN KEENE,	Woodsford, Me.
Mrs. Etta F. C. Kendall,	Auburndale, Mass.
Mrs. Eliza M. C. Kennedy,	Watertown, Mass.
Mr. Horace Kennedy,	Watertown, Mass.
Mrs. Harriet P. Kimball,	Dubuque, Iowa.
Mrs. HELEN M. C. LLOYD,	Chicago, Ill.
Mrs. C. B. McLEAN,	Pittsburg, Pa.
Mrs. FLORENCE CHAMBERLAIN MOSELY,	
	New Haven, Conn.
Mr. JOHN CHAMBERLAIN ORDWAY,	Concord, N. H.
Mrs. Carrie A. C. Oxford,	Eliot, Me.
Mr. George Herbert Perry,	Cambridge, Mass.
Mrs. Minnie A. C. Perry,	Cambridge, Mass.
Mr. Ralph Dana Perry,	Cambridge, Mass.
Mr. JOHN S. RINGWALT, Jr.,	Mt. Vernon, Ohio.
Mrs. C. W. Seymour,	Hingham, Mass.
Mrs. ANNA EUGENIA SMILEY,	Marblehead, Mass.
Rev. E. E. Strong, D. D.,	Auburndale, Mass.
Miss Jennie Chamberlain Watts,	Madison, Wis.
Mrs. MARTHA C. WILSON,	Woodsford, Me.

ASSOCIATE MEMBERS.

Mr. George M. Brown,	Hartford, Conn.
Mr. George B. Caswell,	Cambridgeport, Mass.
Mrs. Alice Rhea Chamberlin,	Torresdale, Pa.
Mrs. Anna Garland Chamberlain,	Andover, Mass.
Mrs. Asa W. Chamberlin,	Jamaica Plain, Mass.
Mrs. Emma B. Chamberlin,	Chicago, Ill.
Mrs. Fannie E. Chamberlin,	Philadelphia, Pa.
Mrs. M. A. Chamberlin,	Greenville, N. H.
Mrs. Newell Chamberlain,	Cambridge, Mass.
Mrs. Robert H. Chamberlain,	Worcester, Mass.
Mrs. Samuel E. Chamberlain,	Barre Plain, Mass.
Mrs. Samuel M. Chamberlain,	Cambridge, Mass.
Mrs. Thomas Chamberlain,	Hyde Park, Mass.
Mr. Albert C. Clarke,	Southbridge, Mass.
Mr. Charles Damon,	Reading, Mass.
Mr. James H. Kendall,	Auburndale, Mass.
***Mr. Frank W. Perry,**	Cambridge, Mass.
(Died June 20, 1898.)	
Mrs. Willard Chamberlain,	Watertown, Mass.

LIFE MEMBERS.

Mrs. Lucy P. Chamberlain,	Medford, Mass.
Rev. L. T. Chamberlain, LL. D.,	
	New York City, N. Y.

Chamberlain Association

... OF ...

AMERICA.

❧

Report of Annual Meeting

HELD IN

BOSTON, SEPTEMBER, 1900.

MELLEN CHAMBERLAIN.

Chamberlain Association

. . . OF . . .

AMERICA.

❧

Report of Annual Meeting

HELD IN

BOSTON, SEPTEMBER, 1900.

The Chamberlain Association of America.

ANNUAL MEETING OF 1900.

IN pursuance of a vote passed last year the Executive Committee selected a later date for the Annual Meeting, and the members were summoned to meet at the Parker House, Boston, on Wednesday, September 19.

The Standing Committees held short sessions in the morning. By 11 o'clock twenty-two members of the Association had gathered in the parlor, and the meeting was called to order by Mr. Montague Chamberlain, in the absence of the President and the Vice-Presidents. He read a letter from the President, General Joshua L. Chamberlain, explaining the latter's absence — he had been attacked suddenly by illness and was unable to be present.

Mr. Jacob Chester Chamberlain was chosen as a temporary Chairman, and Mr. Montague Chamberlain filled the vacancy caused by the absence of Mr. Asa W. Chamberlin, the Recording Secretary.

3

A committee composed of Miss Laura B. Chamberlain and Mr. Montague Chamberlain were requested to send a telegram to the President conveying the regret of the meeting at his enforced absence, and expressing sympathy and hope for a speedy recovery.

The first report read was that of the Recording Secretary, who announced that eighty new members had been admitted during the year, making a total of 234 who have joined the Association. There were three deaths to chronicle : —

Mr. D. C. Bloomer, died February 26, 1900.

Miss N. Augusta Chamberlain, died March 22, 1900.

Hon. Mellen Chamberlain, LL. D., died June 25, 1900.

The Assistant Treasurer read a statement of the receipts and expenditures for the past year, which is printed on another page of this Report.

On motion it was resolved that the reports of the Corresponding Secretary, the Genealogical Committee, the Committee on Colonial and Revolutionary History, and the Committee on English Ancestry be read at the dinner in the evening, instead of at the present meeting.

The Executive Committee, through Mr. Montague Chamberlain, asked the opinion of the meeting regarding a change of the time for the Annual Meeting, and a vote was passed changing the day named in

4

the By-laws to "the last Wednesday in August." Another vote authorized the Executive to arrange the program for the Annual Meeting next year as follows : —

Committees will meet at ten o'clock; at noon, the President will hold a reception, to be followed by a luncheon at one o'clock. After the luncheon has been served, the business of the Association will be taken up, interspersed with informal addresses, music, etc., making one continuous session from noon until the finish — say at five or six o'clock.

At this juncture, Vice-President General Samuel E. Chamberlain entered the room and took the chair. The officers for the ensuing year were then elected, and the business session was closed a little after midday.

At three o'clock about fifty members assembled in the parlor. Vice-President General Samuel E. Chamberlain and his wife received, and the Executive Committee acted as ushers and introduced the strangers, of whom there were a number. The Committee was assisted by Miss Anna P. Chamberlain, Miss Jennie Chamberlain Watts, and Miss Helen Chamberlain.

During the afternoon, Miss Anna P. Chamberlain played on the piano several selections from Chopin and Liszt, and Miss Amy Blanchard read from her story, "A Girl of '76."

The dinner was served in the Crystal Dining-room of Parker's, where twice before the clan Chamberlain had gathered for a similar service. Vice-President General Samuel E. Chamberlain presided, and led the march from the parlor to the cadence of inspiring music furnished by Miss Anna P. Chamberlain. Prayer was offered by the Rev. Dr. E. E. Strong, and without further ceremony the viands were discussed.

The inner man satisfied, the Chairman called the meeting to order and in feeling terms expressed the regret that all felt at the enforced absence of the President. He announced that there was business demanding attention, but to make it less irksome speeches in lighter mood would be sandwiched in between formal reports and serious resolutions. He proposed to demand of each member present something in the way of entertainment.

The first number on the Chairman's program was the report of the Corresponding Secretary, a paper which proved so interesting and valuable that by a unanimous vote the meeting authorized its publication in the Annual Report of the Association. It will be found on another page.

The Rev. Dr. E. E. Strong was next presented and spoke a few words of cordial welcome to the visiting members.

Miss Laura B. Chamberlain was introduced as a returned missionary to Armenia and delivered a speech of welcome in the language of that country.

Mr. Montague Chamberlain was described as "the only native American present," and he responded in an Indian dialect, welcoming the pale-faces to the old hunting ground of their red-skinned brothers.

The Treasurer, Mr. Thomas Chamberlain, read a letter from Colonel Thomas Chamberlin, of Philadelphia, explaining that ill health prevented him attending the gathering, which led to a vote that a telegram conveying the regrets and sympathy of the meeting be sent to the gallant and popular Colonel.

The report of the Genealogical Committee was read by Mr. George W. Chamberlain, the Bureau Secretary, who read also the report of the Committee on English Ancestry. Both were accepted with applause, and the Executive Committee was instructed to publish them.

Miss Abbie M. Chamberlain read the report of the Committee on Colonial and Revolutionary History. A vote was passed ordering the publication of the report and expressing the obligation of the Society to the compiler, Dr. J. W. Chamberlain.

7

The Chairman announced the death of three members during the year, and asked Miss Laura B. Chamberlain to read a note in memoriam of Judge Mellen Chamberlain that had been prepared by a committee appointed by the President. The members stood while the paper was being read.

IN MEMORIAM.

Since our last meeting it has pleased our Divine Father to remove from us

MELLEN CHAMBERLAIN,

an interested and honored member of the Association, and its senior Vice-President. Although for a few years past partially restrained from active service by impaired health, yet his interest in every high cause was undiminished.

His residence during the last portion of his life was in Chelsea, Mass., close to the land belonging to his ancestor, Jacob Chamberlain, one of the original settlers of Chelsea.

He graduated at Dartmouth College and Harvard Law School, and in the maturity of his years received from his Alma Mater the high degree of Honorary Doctor of Laws, in token of his distinguished ability and learning. He filled very important positions of usefulness in municipal and legislative service for

8

many years,—a fact which testifies to the confidence and honor in which he was held by his fellow citizens. He served with distinction in both branches of the General Court of Massachusetts, was Chief Justice of the Municipal Court of Boston, and for twelve years Superintendent of her Public Library. American Colonial and Revolutionary History was the field of some of his most important labors, and in this his judicial habit of mind and his historic sense made him one of the leading authorities. His force and clearness as a writer gave him high rank among American authors. His collections of manuscripts, autographs and rare historical documents is one of the most choice and valuable to be found in the country.

He was a member of the New Hampshire and Massachusetts Historical Societies, and corresponding member of the Royal Society of Northern Antiquities at Copenhagen, Denmark.

Besides these wider and more conspicuous services Judge Chamberlain was actively connected with various local organizations in Chelsea, Mass., where he resided for over half a century,—a Selectman of the Town, and Alderman of the City, member of the School Committee, City Solicitor, Commissioner of the Sinking Fund, Trustee of the Chelsea Public Library, and Park Commissioner. He was a principal bene-factor of the Congregational Church in Chelsea, of which he was a member, and where he will be greatly missed.

He has passed from us full of years and honors, in the peace of a deep trust in the acceptance of Christ, his Saviour.

Be it therefore resolved:

That the members of this Association recognize the high character and eminent public services of Judge Mellen Chamberlain, and with cherished remembrance of his endearing personal qualities, desire to inscribe upon the records of this Association this token of their profound respect and affection; and that they tender to his kindred and friends their sorrowing sympathy, with the trust that the afterglow of his name may be, for generations to come, an inspiration to patriotism and to fidelity in every public duty.

Mr. Montague Chamberlain drew the attention of the members to the valuable and generous assistance that had been rendered to the Association by Rev. Dr. Leander T. Chamberlain, of New York. Dr. Chamberlain has been an active worker on the Bureau Directorate, as well as zealous in the department of English Ancestry, of which Committee he is Chairman. He has also contributed generously towards the expenses, and has presented the Genealogical Bureau with a safe in which to keep the MSS.

Reference was also made to the important and extended work in the interests of the Association that has been performed by the Corresponding Secretary, Miss Abbie M. Chamberlain, who has proved herself both zealous and efficient, as well as untiring. But for her zeal and enthusiasm and energy, the Association could not have attained its present prosperous condition. This reference to the genial and popular Secretary was received with prolonged applause.

Speeches were made by General Robert H. Chamberlain, of Worcester, Mass., Mr. William Chamberlain, of Portland, Maine, and Mr. Charles W. Chamberlain, of Dayton, Ohio.

The Chairman announced that he had hoped to meet at this year's gathering a distinguished clansman, the Rev. Dr. Jacob Chamberlain, father of the energetic Chairman of the Genealogical Committee. Dr. Chamberlain has labored for many years as a missionary in India, and is now home for a brief respite. He anticipated attending this reunion, but was detained in New York, as the following letter explains:

To THE CHAMBERLAIN ASSOCIATION,
    In Session in Boston, September 19th, 1900.

Clansmen.—Your Hindu kinsman sends most affectionate greetings, and sincere regrets that imperative duty in New York on the 19th instant prevents his attendance at the rallying of the Clan in Boston on the same day, especially as he is just turning his pale face once more back to the land where he and his companion have delved and sowed and reaped for the last forty-one years.

That you may see that his delving, as well as his sowing and reaping, has at least been interesting, he sends you herewith a few gems that he has dug up from an old Hindu Farmer Poet, who wrote in India, in his beautiful foreign language, some 800 years ago. The Telugu poetry he has endeavored to translate into the same metre and flow as in the original, that the spirit and the life of this poetry may be seen. Only a few select verses are transcribed.

Vernana, the Telugu poet of the twelfth century, sang thus:

The excellent upon this earth are rarely found,
The base and vile abound look where you will,
To find a golden nugget one seeks far,
But rubbish lies beneath your feet where'er you go.

The words which from the lips of wise men drop
Are sweet as warblings of the nightingale,
But worse than cawing of the wretched crow
Are the unceasing words of empty-headed men.

The simple head that holds but little sense
Is always talking and with loudest noise,
The learned sage speaks softly, and with fewer words;
Bell-metal gives a louder sound than gold.

The property I make and keep is all my own, you say,
But fools alone agree with you and say 'tis so:
O man, the wealth thou giv'st in charity alone is thine,
For that alone will follow thee to yonder world.

No need of poison if a miser you would kill,
A cheaper and a surer method you can find,
Just ask him for some pence to give the poor,
And shocked, and troubled, down he falls and dies.

Beware! where the gods do dwell, you wildly shout,
And journey there with great desire and toil and cash,
But is not here the God that's there?   If with the heart
    you seek Him,
He's here, He's there, He's everywhere,— go where you
    will, you meet Him.

'Tis not by roaming deserts wild, nor gazing at the sky,
'Tis not by battling in the stream, nor pilgrimage to
    shrine,
But thine own heart must thou make pure, and then and
    then alone
Shalt thou see Him no eye hath kenned: shalt thou
    behold thy King.

These few selections from this old Hindu poet will
show that the people to whose Christian elevation
your kinsman has devoted his life are a most interesting people, with capabilities of understanding the
highest truths, and who are worth working for to help
up to that for which their higher spirits have long
been yearning, that with the aid which the revealed

13

word of God contains they may indeed be able at length to "behold their King."

Your kinsman and brother,
JACOB CHAMBERLAIN.

A hearty vote of thanks expressed the feelings of those present towards the genial and witty soldier-brother who had presided, and General Samuel E. Chamberlain modestly bowed his acknowledgment.

Then the company arose and joined hands while they sang "America" and "Auld Lang Syne," and the Third Annual Meeting was finished.

REPORT OF THE CORRESPONDING
SECRETARY.

The atmosphere of the second Annual Meeting of the Chamberlain Association was tonic with hope and anticipation, for the presence of a majority of the Vice-Presidents and of the members of the various committees at the business session in the morning of September 8th, 1899, was indicative of a deepening interest in the success of the Society. The present meeting was projected at that time.

Last year there was an enthusiastic gathering at the reception held in the afternoon, when the "paramount issue" seemed to be good fellowship and social intercourse. The occasion was thought to be something more than "the flowering of people's enthusiasm," and many felt that the best fruitage of the study of ancestry was the social side. In the evening, "the family" realized that dinner added zest to sociability, and the program held a sustained interest throughout.

The founding of the Genealogical Bureau, through the generosity of three gentlemen, Dr. L. T. Chamberlain, Mr. Jacob Chester Chamberlain and Hon. D. H. Chamberlain, brought joy to all hearts, for there is a general desire to have a Chamberlain genealogy published. Fortunately the Bureau secretary has not been called upon "to walk through a graveyard of slaughtered reputations," in his study of American ancestry, for generally the fore-bears of our clan were good exponents of New England thought, thrift and industry, their heritage from good English Puritan ancestors. The pioneers of the family were regal with the splendid toil of daily life and work.

Dr. O. W. Holmes said, "Science is a good piece of furniture for a man to have in an upper chamber, provided he has common sense on the ground floor." The Chamberlains seem to have been well established on the ground floor, and in later days have apparently mounted to the upper chambers, judging from the numerous A. B.'s, LL. B.'s, Ph. D.'s, LL. D.'s, D. D.'s, and M. D.'s attached to the members' names. Not all have acquired a fervid interest in genealogy, for some hesitate about tracing streams to a source which might run muddy, or fear that a Paul Pry may discover some reprobates in their family line. The Bible abounds in genealogies of tribes and families, though the men of Bible days were not always perfect. We Chamberlains expect to be exceptions to all rules, but we have yet to learn that there ever was an Abel or a Judas in our tribe, while we do know that the Jacobs, Joshuas, Samuels, and Benjamins have been numerous in their generations. The Bible was their text-book, dictionary and guide.

To the oft repeated question, Has your Society adopted a coat-of-arms yet? we reply that we still remain on the threshold of that subject. Burke in his book, "The General Armory," and Fairburn in his works give so many crests of the different English Chamberlains,—'lins and 'laynes,—that we have not yet attempted to decide upon any one. We await further researches in English ancestry. A Western writer in the *New England Magazine* has a very original and suggestive device for a coat-of-arms for New Englanders,—"No more significant emblem could be incorporated in the device than an ordinary stone-wall; for it tells of the long and heroic battle with obstacles by which our New England fathers redeemed the land and at the same time acquired a vigor of manhood, which gave them a controlling hand in the destinies of the nation." This writer had lived on a Western prairie farm for over twenty years; hence his appreciation of stone walls!

The *esprit-de-corps* amongst the officers and members of our Society has been most excellent during the past year. We note with pleasure the large increase in numbers, especially from the middle West. During the past year we have admitted members from Kansas, Missouri, North Dakota, California, North and South Carolina, and now have on our roll representatives of twenty-nine states, the District of Columbia and the Hawaiian Islands. Our President has an

17

international fame, and our society seems to be becoming so, for we have members in England, India, Brazil and Buenos Ayres. This organization already constitutes a large society, but if each one now on the roll should feel inspired to bring in a new member, what a mammoth Association we should become!

If additional funds could be added to our treasury by membership, or otherwise, it would hasten the completion of the Chamberlain genealogy; with increased means, the scope and breadth of the work could be enlarged. Owing to the wide separation of the members of our committees, it has been difficult for all to engage with such active interest and personal coöperation as they have desired, but we acknowledge with gratitude the spirit of helpfulness which has actuated those who have striven to extend the interests of the Association.

The first important fruit of investigations in Colonial and Revolutionary History is the Report of the Chairman, Dr. J. W. Chamberlain, which was received with surprise and delight. Few states have yet published a complete list of their Colonial and Revolutionary soldiers, hence the difficulty in obtaining an accurate roll, but Dr. Chamberlain, with characteristic energy, has gathered all that was available. This list may require some slight revision, and it is hoped that all errors or omissions may be reported, as it is a notable record of the patriotism and loyalty of the Chamberlains, in responding to the call of the country.

We are much indebted also to Dr. William R. Chamberlain, of Washington, D. C., for generously presenting the Association with a classified list of the Revolutionary pensioners bearing our name, from the New England States. The data for this list was drawn from the original records in Washington, and forms a timely and valuable gift.

The society is under an obligation to Mr. Montague Chamberlain for editing and supervising through the press the annual reports. These documents reflect much credit upon our society; and we trust that our members will see that copies are placed in the Libraries of the cities and towns in which they reside. The chairmen of the various committees, as well as our Treasurer, Assistant Treasurer, and other officers, are entitled to our thanks for so faithfully and loyally giving time and labor to promote the interest of the society.*

All are volunteers, willingly and loyally serving under our heroic commander and President, whom we have so much missed to-day. Nor can we forget our efficient Vice-Presidents,—may they be long spared to us.

---

*To none of its officers or members is the Association under such deep obligation as to the Corresponding Secretary herself.— *Editor.*

Our sympathies have been especially enlisted for that brave soldier and accomplished gentleman, Vice-President Colonel Thomas Chamberlain, of Philadelphia, who won a large place in our hearts at last year's Annual Meeting. For months past he has been a great sufferer, in which I am sure all will extend him their sympathy.

It was a very happy thought of some of our Western members to send us their photographs, when unable to be present. In this way we can welcome at our festival this year Professor Paul Mellen Chamberlain and family of Chicago, and Dr. G. M. Chamberlain. We are also indebted to Professor William B. Chamberlain and Rev. James A. Chamberlain for pictures sent last year.

This Association holds its meetings in the old city of Boston, the first home of some of the pioneers, but it knows no party affiliations, no sectionalism; there are no types of social feeling seeking to find an equilibrium in the social conditions of the various branches; but its members are expected to subscribe to the principles of good sterling Americanism, and to civic virtues for its own welfare.

From the evangel of "the little red school-house" has blossomed out great ideas and thoughts in the twentieth century, so we have the commerce of intellect and the currency of thought,— which passes from one country to another. The Chamberlains can claim their share in the world's literature, for we find the name in encyclopædias and catalogues of books. This doubtless suggested a thought to our Western cousins, "that we should compile a list of the names of authors and of their works, to be appended to the forthcoming Chamberlain book." It is evident that they believe in expansion even in a family society.

The New England element are talking about observing "Old Home Week" for an anniversary, and in this connection it may be well to refer to a mooted question, Shall we have annual or bi-annual sessions hereafter? Or shall we have a more informal gathering in the day-time?

In conclusion permit me to remark that the Association seems to be in a prosperous and flourishing condition. We appreciate the loyalty of our charter members as evidenced by their attendance at these Anniversaries, and in their name we welcome those who have honored us with their presence for the first time at this gathering. Nor must I omit a word of personal thanks to distant members for their interesting and encouraging letters. May we not hope that we shall have the pleasure of seeing them also face to face in the near future.

Submitted with cordial greetings,
ABBIE MELLEN CHAMBERLAIN,
Corresponding Secretary.

REPORT OF THE GENEALOGICAL COMMITTEE.

In their last report this Committee outlined a plan for the development of an increased interest in the Chamberlain Association, and the hearty coöperation of several members has led to the organization of a Genealogical Bureau as the working part of this Committee.

Our report this year will therefore be offered through the Bureau, but we desire to refer again to the purpose of the Bureau's existence, briefly stated in the leaflet mailed to members last year, *i. e.*, to centralize and simplify researches into Chamberlain genealogy and to have these researches available to our members.

The report of the Bureau will show that the members have been classified with respect to their most remote ancestor. Many have been traced to Richard, Thomas, Edmund and William, whom we class as progenitors. Others in groups have been traced to Jacob, Lewis, Joseph and Wright, who are not known to have been immigrants to this country.

We now hope that the members in these several groups may either individually carry the connecting links back further or unite in having the researches made; but here let us say that every fee charged by the Bureau's Secretary to cover work done for individual members is credited to the treasury of the Bureau to further general research, as your Committee has arranged for the maintenance of the Bureau by private subscription.

As the researches progress we may all be linked as a large family through the few original immigrants or progenitors known to have brought our name to these shores. There we leave the work for the Committee on English Ancestry, who will carry us back to the Old Country, and into problems perhaps even more perplexing.

J. C. CHAMBERLAIN,
Chairman.

REPORT OF THE GENEALOGICAL BUREAU.

At the last Annual Meeting of this Association the Genealogical Committee was authorized to establish a Bureau of Genealogy. As Secretary of that Bureau I have the honor to submit my first report.

This Bureau has attempted to carry on four kinds of work for the Association during the year, *viz.:*

To reply to all genealogical inquiries from the members of the Association.

To collect and classify genealogical information to the end that a "Chamberlain Genealogy" may be completed.

23

To make investigations concerning the ancestry of individual members at their special request.

To trace the ancestry of every member of our Association to a remote or immigrant Chamberlain ancestor and record the same in the Genealogical Bureau Record.

The Bureau has sent out during the year nearly 450 letters. It has received the following valuable MSS. donations, for which thanks are hereby returned:

The Family Record of Lewis Chamberlin, of New Jersey (1709–1819).

The Caswell Collection of Chamberlain Deaths (1788–1895).

The Chamberlain Families, of Kent, Conn. (1737–1862).

Jacob Chamberlain's Family, of Dudley, Mass. (1744–1899).

Descendants of Peleg Chamberlain, of Connecticut (1736–1887).

Descendants of Lemuel Chamberlain, of Massachusetts (1754–1879).

A Family History, prepared before 1849 by the late Levi Chamberlain, of Honolulu, Hawaii.

The Family Record of William Chamberlain, of Connecticut (1754–1898).

Male Descendants of Joseph Chamberlain, of Colchester, Conn.

The Secretary has prepared since the first day of September, 1899, MSS. for use in the Bureau as follows:

A revised and enlarged copy of "The Descendants of Thomas Chamberlain, Woburn, 1644," of 26 pages.

An outline of the Descendants of Richard Chamberlin, of Roxbury, giving from three to five generations (1642–1750), and of 30 pages.

The early movements of the Chamberlain Immigrants in America (1635–1656), of 7 pages.

A complete Index to "One Branch of the Descendants of Thomas Chamberlain, Woburn, 1644," containing 358 names, and of 9 pages.

An outline of the Descendants of Edmund Chamberlain, of Chelmsford and Roxbury, giving four generations (1647–1750), and of 26 pages.

An outline of the Chamberlain Families of Colchester, Conn. (1705–1756), of 9 pages.

A calendar of Chamberlain Deeds in New Hampshire (1729–1800), of 6 pages.

An Index to the Descendants of William Chamberlain, of Billerica, Mass.

These researches and compilations are along the line of the progenitors as classified in previous reports and as listed on our leaflet.

The Bureau acknowledges with many thanks having received during the year the following published material:

Sketch of the Life of Hon. Mellen Chamberlain, LL. D., of Chelsea, Mass.

"Genealogical Record of the Chemberlin Family" (1883), 24 pages. Compiled and published by John Wilson Chamberlin, Tiffin, Ohio.

A Reprint of the "Report of the Chamberlain Association for 1899."

A Reprint of the "President's Address, Chamberlain Association Meeting of 1898."

A Reprint of "Sketch of Rev. Leander Trowbridge Chamberlain."

"Amy E. Blanchard" (Autobiographical) in *Book News* for July, 1900.

Historical Sketch of "Brookfield and West Brookfield," Mass. By the Hon. Daniel H. Chamberlain, LL. D., and in the *New England Magazine* for December, 1899.

These lists, however, constitute only a small part of the material which is now in the possession of the Secretary.

The Bureau has responded to calls for special investigation from individual members and is preparing work already authorized by other members.

A scientific study of the ancestry of the members

26

of this Association was the far-reaching thought of your Committee in the establishment of this Bureau. To accomplish that end they furnished the Secretary with a Genealogical Bureau Record — a book of 400 pages so constructed that opposite the enrollment of every member's name his ancestral line can be recorded backward through ten consecutive generations. To increase our facilities for gaining the desired information, it is necessary that each new member shall fill out a genealogical blank and return the same to the Bureau Secretary. Here are the results:

Of the 225 members enrolled to September 1, 1900, nineteen are Associate Members, the "better halves" of the Association. There are, therefore, 206 members who are fit subjects for genealogical diagnosis. The goal for each member is to discover and to rehabilitate that remote and immigrant ancestor bearing the surname Chamberlain who left the familiar scenes of the Old World for the hardships and privations of the New. No member has yet been traced to Leonard Chamberlayne of Virginia, 1637, to Henry Chamberlain of Hingham, Mass., 1638, or to Robert or Jonas Chamberlain of Pennsylvania,— all immigrants who left descendants.

Among our members 84 have been traced to their immigrant ancestor as follows:

Four to Richard Chamberlin, of Braintree, 1642.

Three to Thomas Chamberlain, of Woburn, 1644.

Six to Edmund Chamberlain, of Roxbury, 1647.

Forty-seven to William Chamberlain, of Woburn, 1648.

Eleven to Jacob Chamberlain, of Chelsea, about 1720.

Eleven to Lewis Chamberlin, of New Jersey, about 1735.

Two to Samuel Chamberlaine, of Maryland, about 1735.

In the unclassified, disconnected branches now traced back from three to five or six generations, I find 68 members. There is still another class — a class that I call "unancestored" — containing 55 members, *i. e.*, those who have returned no report even as to their father. Shall we not receive a genealogical blank filled out from these 55 members?

This Bureau would appreciate the coöperation of every member and would be glad to receive every Chamberlain family record and so become an ever-increasing repository of family history. We ought to have all Chamberlain data to be found in the county, town and parish records of certain localities, notably of Woodstock and Colchester in Connecticut and of Monmouth and Hunterdon counties in New Jersey. Are there not a score of members "tied up" in these respective localities who are willing and able to combine and authorize a thorough search for and collection of all Chamberlain data in these localities, that their ancestral lines may be definitely established?

In conclusion the members of this Association are to be congratulated upon their selection of such wise and able organizers in the Genealogical Committee — organizers who have successfully established a Bureau of Genealogy at once unique, and so far as I have the means of knowing, the first of its kind to exist in America for a family Association.

Respectfully submitted,

GEORGE W. CHAMBERLAIN,

Bureau Secretary.

PROGENITORS OF THE CHAMBERLAIN FAMILIES IN AMERICA.

LEONARD CHAMBERLAYNE — came to Virginia early in the year 1637 in a ship commanded by Captain William Frye. Captain Leonard Chamberlayne, supposed to be the same man, received a patent of 650 acres of land in New Kent County, Virginia, in 1657. This patent was renewed to his son Leonard in 1662. From the earliest times the New Kent County families have invariably spelled the surname Chamberlayne.

HENRY CHAMBERLIN — first appears in Hingham, Mass., in 1638, having come from the parish of Hingham, County Norfolk, England, in the ship "Diligent," with his wife Jane, his mother Christian and two children. He was one of many who, under the leadership of Rev. Robert Peck, fled from the religious persecution of that time. In the same year he had land granted him by the town of Hingham and was made a Freeman, 13 March, 1638-9. Some time after 1661 Henry Chamberlin, with his family, removed to the adjoining town of Hull, Mass., where he died 15 July, 1674.

His descendants of the earlier generations lived in Boston, Charlestown, Scituate, Bridgewater, Hanover and Hadley, Mass., Newport, R. I., Shrewsbury, N. J., and Dorchester, S. C.

RICHARD CHAMBERLIN — is first known as of Braintree in 1642, being thus referred to in Boston town records of that date. He removed to Roxbury, where, on the "4th day, 4th month (June), 1665," five of his children were baptized by the Rev. John Eliot, the Apostle of the Indians, at his church in Roxbury. At this time Richard Chamberlin's house and lot in Roxbury were adjoining that of John Eliot. About 1668 he removed to Sudbury and died before 15 April, 1673, on which date his will of February 12th preceding was probated.

The earlier generations of his descendants lived in Sudbury, Oxford, Dudley and Northfield, Mass., Colchester and Hebron, Conn., Chesterfield, N. H., and Newbury, Vt.

THOMAS CHAMBERLAIN — first appears in New England at Woburn, Mass., where he was made a Freeman by the General Court, 29 May, 1644. He was the principal proprietor of the Dudley Grant in Billerica, Mass. He does not seem to have settled there, and subsequently gave deeds for parts of his Dudley Grant to William and Edmund Chamberlain and others; he was one of the earliest settlers of Chelmsford, being referred to in 1654 as of Chelmsford, where he lived until his death, probably before the 21st of December, 1700.

His descendants lived in Chelmsford, Westford, Littleton, Groton and Pepperell, Mass., Lyndeborough and Merrimack, N. H., Cavendish, Vt., Waterford, Gardiner and Hallowell, Me.

31

EDMUND CHAMBERLAIN — first appears in New England at Roxbury, where he married Mary Turner, 4 January, 1646-7. He appears to have moved frequently, for he was living at Woburn in 1649, when his daughter Sarah was born, and in 1654 at Billerica, where he settled a farm adjoining the land of William Chamberlain. On the 22d of October, 1655, in a deed he styles himself as a "planter" of Chelmsford, where he remained until after the death of his wife Sarah, in Roxbury, 7 January, 1669. He married again, 22 June, 1670, at Chelmsford, but soon he removed to Malden, and on the 27th of October, 1678, he was a resident of Roxbury, having that day deeded his Chelmsford farm, bounded by Thomas Chamberlain's farm. With a company of Roxbury people, Edmund and his son of the same name removed to New Roxbury (now Woodstock, Conn.), where he died on May 8, 1696.

His early descendants lived in Roxbury, Malden, Chelsea, Mass., and Woodstock, Conn.

WILLIAM CHAMBERLAIN — is first known in New England in 1648, having been admitted as an inhabitant of the town of Woburn, Mass., on the 6th of January. He was one of the incorporators and original settlers of Billerica, Mass., in 1654, and lived there till his death, 31 May, 1706.

His wife Rebecca was accused of being a witch and confined in the prison at Cambridge, where she died, 26 September, 1692 — only a few months before the witchcraft delusion ended.

His descendants lived in Billerica, Cambridge, Newton, Brookline, Charlestown, Holliston, Worcester, Westborough and New Marlborough, Mass., and Rochester, N. H., and Lebanon and Orrington, Me.

REPORT OF THE COMMITTEE ON ENGLISH ANCESTRY.

To the Rev. Leander Trowbridge Chamberlain, D. D., *Chairman.*

Dear Sir,— I beg to submit the following report of what has been accomplished in the department of English Ancestry for the year ending September 1, 1900.

The Bureau has attempted to carry forward two lines of work, *viz.:* (1) To make a general collection of data from published sources relating to the English families of the surname Chamberlain and its variants; and (2) to direct independent, original researches in the most promising localities of England. Following is the

GENERAL COLLECTION IN MSS.

Bibliography of Publications Relating to the English Chamberlain Families, twelve pages.

Clews to the Emigrant Chamberlains of New England, ten pages.

Musgrave's Obituary of Chamberlains, seven pages, giving brief mention of sixty-four Chamberlains who died in England, Scotland, or Ireland between 1375 and 1800, together with full references to more extended published accounts of them.

Complete Bibliography of English Parish Registers
published in whole or in part and to be found
in the Library of the New England Historic
Genealogical Society of Boston, five hundred
and seventy registers.

Gleanings from the visitations of Cambridge, Suffolk
and Norfolk. These gleanings indicate a common origin of the families here described at
Stoke-by-Nayland in the County of Suffolk.

Memoranda relating to English Chamberlains, fifty
pages.

THE ORIGINAL RESEARCHES

have for the following reasons been confined largely
to the Counties of Essex, Suffolk and Norfolk:—
(1) Among the neighbors of the Chamberlain immigrants to New England were many who came from the
territory lying between the Thames and the Wash;
(2) the New England Chamberlain immigrants — one
of whom appears to have been prominently identified
with the settlement and incorporation of Chelmsford
in Massachusetts — settled in towns having the same
names as the towns within this territory; and (3)
the statement of the eminent historian, Dr. John
Fiske, that "probably two-thirds of the American
people who can trace their ancestry to New England
might follow it back to the East Anglian shires of
the mother-country."—(Fiske's "The Beginnings of
New England," pp. 62–65.)

Following is a statement of the researches in detail:

An examination of twenty-six Parish Registers in the Counties of Essex and Suffolk, made by the parish rectors and clerks under the direction of one of our members, A. C. Allen Chamberlain, Esquire, of Winchester, Mass., during the summer of 1899, and by him generously donated to this Association.

A Calendar of all Chamberlain Wills for Ireland (1604–1880). Donated to the Association by another member, John Wilson Chamberlin, Esquire, of Tiffin, Ohio, thirty-seven wills.

An examination of every probate court having jurisdiction (1620 to 1670) within the Counties of Essex, Suffolk and Norfolk. For this period the Chamberlain wills found on file and calendared for our Bureau are as follows:

In the Prerogative Court of Canterbury .	43
In the Commissary Court of London .	7
In the Archdeaconry Court of Colchester .	6
In the Archdeaconry Court of Essex . .	6
In the Peculiar Royal Court of Westminster	2
In the Archdeaconry Court of Sudbury .	3
In the Consistory Court of Norwich . .	5
In the Archdeaconry Court of Suffolk .	4
In the Archdeaconry Court of Norfolk .	5
Total	81

Abstracts of Wills and Administrations from the Calendars of the above-named courts:

1626, Richard Chamberlyn, of Framlingham.
1626, Sir Thomas Chamberlaine, of Banbary.
1630, Thomas Chamberlaine, of Tadley.
1630, William Chamberlaine, of East Deerham.
1632, William Chamberlyne, of Royston.
1632, John Camberlyne, of Beaumond.
1632–33, Thomas Chamberlyn, of Bradwell.
1634, Thomas Chamberlyn, of Dunston.
1636, William Chamberlayne, at sea.
1638, Thomas Chamberlain, of Stratford in Suffolk.
1642, Thomas Chamberlayne, of Hapisburg.
1645, Thomas Chamberline, of Lambourne.
1651, William Chamberlaine, of Swaffham.
1661, Thomas Chamberlyne, of Banham.
1664, Thomas Chamberlain, of Wilby.
1665, Thomas Chamberlaine, of Cockfield.
1666, John Chamberlin, of Great Bromly.
1666, Thomas Chamberlaine, alias Janvrin, of Stepney.
1667, Thomas Chamberlain, of Elmsted.
1667, Thomas Chamberlaine, of St. Margaret.

To recapitulate, these researches show that fourteen courts have been examined for Chamberlain wills; and that in nine of these courts we found such wills on file to the number of eighty-one. We have had these calendared and the calendars forwarded to the Bureau. From our calendars we have selected twenty from which we have secured abstracts containing family relationships that are of great value. To the genealogist the material is invaluable for the clews furnished.

Respectfully submitted,

GEORGE W. CHAMBERLAIN,

Bureau Secretary.

REPORT OF COMMITTEE ON COLONIAL AND REVOLUTIONARY ANCESTRY.

Mr. President and Members of the Chamberlain Association:

On this, the Third Annual Meeting of our Association, I have the honor to submit herewith the first report your Committee on Colonial and Revolutionary Ancestry has been able to make. It has been my firm intention each year to be present with you on the occasion of the Annual Meeting, but each year I have been unable to meet with you for various reasons, which seemed to me were paramount in their importance. I have had some correspondence with other members of the Committee and with some of our name outside of the Committee, but they have seemingly been so situated that they could not afford much assistance.

The report which I herewith submit to you does not go into details of the services rendered by each man named, as it would have been a Herculean task to have compiled such a mass of history. I started out with that idea, but very soon found that I would not have the time to complete the work, nor would this Association feel like giving the time to listen to such a voluminous report. I have therefore contented myself with giving a tabulated statement of the different men of our name who served the Colonies, either in a civil or military capacity, and those who were soldiers in the War of the Revolution. If any member of the Association desires a more extended account regarding the residence or the services rendered by any of those whom I have mentioned, the information thus desired can be procured and I will be very glad to arrange for any who wish to avail themselves of such opportunity.

It is interesting to note that our name is found spelled in many different ways, which are all to be found in the early records of the Colonies. There are in the lists from the different Colonies and States many with the same given name, and fearing lest some of these might be duplicates, I have had the ground gone carefully over by an expert genealogist, to make sure that each name represented a different individual and not one who might have enlisted several times in the same war, from different localities. For instance, in Massachusetts, there were ten in the Revolution by the name of Benjamin, though their places of enlistment were different. To the best of my knowledge and belief, these were ten different individuals.

I find in the aggregate a grand total of two hundred and ninety-seven, which the schedules of this report will show are divided into those serving the Colonies in a civil capacity, those serving the Colonies in a military capacity, and those who were soldiers in the Revolutionary War.

The only record I could find of those serving in a civil capacity was in New Hampshire, where there were only three: Richard, who was Secretary of the Province; John, who was Deputy to the General Court, and Samuel, also Deputy to the General Court. There were also in New Hampshire, John, who was a Captain of the Militia, and John, a Lieutenant of the Militia. That represents those of our name who served their country during the Colonial period in New Hampshire, but when the Revolutionary War came, our family was much more in evidence. The records show that forty-seven Chamberlains who took part in the Revolution were residents of New Hampshire. Of this number, seven were officers, one a drummer, and the rest privates.

In Massachusetts I have no record of any who served the Colonies in a civil capacity, but there were fifteen who were soldiers of that period, all of whom took part in King Philip's War. The Chamberlains in Massachusetts were not lacking in patriotism when the War of the Revolution broke out, and indeed, it would be difficult to understand how any one so near the Boston Tea Party could have lacked in either patriotism or enthusiasm. Suffice it to say that one hundred and fifty-two of the soldiers who enlisted from Massachusetts bore the name of Chamberlain.

Of those, twenty-five were officers, five musicians, one first lieutenant of marines, and one seaman on the brigantine " Massachusetts."

Those who served in the Colonial Wars in Connecticut numbered ten, and Connecticut should be proud of the fact that not a private soldier was among the number. There was one captain, three were lieutenants, three quartermasters, two ensigns, and one was a musician; a record not to be equalled by any other Colony. There were thirty-one Chamberlains who enlisted in the War of the Revolution from Connecticut, and the percentage of officers to privates ranks exceptionally high; of the thirty-one who enlisted eleven were officers.

It seems that our progenitors were more closely allied with the New England Colonies than with those further west, as there were only four from the State of New York who took part in the Colonial Wars, and in the Revolutionary War there were twelve who served the State in a military capacity, five of whom were officers.

New Jersey rather outstripped New York in her contribution of Chamberlains to the struggles of the early days. While she did not furnish any for the Colonial Wars, there were twenty-three who took part in the War of the Revolution, showing that our family was more largely represented in New Jersey than in New York.

The only other State where I have been able to find a record of Chamberlains in the Revolution is Maryland, and the records state there was a Brigadier-General, James Chamberlaine, who was in the Maryland Militia in 1776. This completes the different divisions as I have outlined them, and by reference to the succeeding lists, this information will be found in detail.

If this report covers at least a portion of the ground which the Association desired to have investigated, I shall feel fully repaid for any labor devoted to it. I am free to confess that I scarcely knew exactly what sort of a report to make, but concluded to report, as nearly as possible, the name, residence and official capacity in which every Chamberlain served his country, either in Colonial or Revolutionary times.

Should you desire any elaboration of this idea, and will be kind enough to make me acquainted with just what you desire, I will be very glad to perform the pleasant duty to the best of my ability. Again regretting my inability to be with you on this occasion, wishing the Association God-speed, and hoping the occasion may be one of great interest and pleasure to each one fortunate enough to be present, I have the honor to submit this report.

Cordially and respectfully,

JEHIEL WESTON CHAMBERLAIN.

REGISTER OF MEMBERS OF THE CHAMBERLAIN FAMILIES WHO SERVED THE AMERICAN COLONIES IN THE COLONIAL AND REVOLUTIONARY PERIODS.

In the original records the name appears in the following forms:*

Camberlain.	Chamberland.	Chamblen.
Camblin.	Chamberlein.	Chamblin.
Chamberlain.	Chamberlene.	Chambling.
Chaimberlain.	Chamberlin.	Chamborlin.
Chaimberlen.	Chamberline.	Chambely.
Chambelen.	Chamberling.	Charmbelain.
Chamberlan.	Chamberlon.	Chombelin.
Chamberlen.	Chambelin.	Chormbelin.
	Chambilen.	

Members of the Chamberlain family in New Hampshire who served the Colony in the Colonial period:

CIVIL.

1. Richard, Secretary of the Province.
2. John, Deputy to the General Court.
3. Samuel, Deputy to the General Court.

---

*The Editor has added a few names taken from the Massachusetts record of soldiers and sailors in the War of the Revolution, Vol. III, p. 251.

4. John, Captain, New Hampshire Militia.
5. John, Lieutenant, New Hampshire Militia.

Members of the Chamberlain family in New Hampshire who served in the Revolution:

	Christian name.	Residence.	Rank.
1.	Aaron,	New Ipswich,	Private.
2.	Abner,		Private.
3.	Abiel,	Canterbury,	Private.
4.	Asher,		Private.
5.	Amasa,		Private.
6.	Asa,		Private.
7.	Benjamin,		Private.
8.	Benjamin,	Cornish,	Private.
9.	Benjamin,	Winchester,	Drummer.
10.	Calvin,		Private.
11.	Daniel,		Private.
12.	David,		Private.
13.	Ebenezer,		Lieutenant.
14.	Ebenezer,		Private.
15.	Ebenezer,	Westmoreland,	Private.
16.	Elias,		Private.
17.	Ephraim,		Lieutenant.
18.	Ephraim,		Private.
19.	Ephraim,	Sanbornton,	Private.
20.	Francis,	Epping,	Private.
21.	Henry,		Private.
22.	Henry,	Westmoreland,	Private.
23.	Ichabod,		Private.

Christian Name.	Residence.	Rank.
24. Ichabod,		Private.
25. Ichabod,		Private.
26. Increase,		Private.
27. Jacob,		Private.
28. Jacob,		Corporal.
29. James,		Corporal.
30. James,	Rochester,	Private.
31. Jason,		Private.
32. Jason,	Rochester,	Private.
33. John,		Private.
34. John,	Fitzwilliam,	Private.
35. Jonathan,	Lyndborough,	Private.
36. Jonathan, Jr.,	Lyndborough,	Private.
37. Moses,		Lieutenant.
38. Moses,		Private.
39. Nathaniel,		Private.
40. Richard,		Private.
41. Samuel,		Private.
42. Samuel, Jr.,	Canterbury,	Lieutenant.
43. Samuel,	Canterbury,	Private.
44. Silas,		Private.
45. Thomas,		Private.
46. William,	Loudon,	Sergeant.
47. William,		Private.

Members of the Chamberlain family in Massachusetts who served in King Philip's war:*

Christian Name.	Residence.	Rank.
1. Benjamin,	Hadley,	Private.
2. Edmund,	Malden,	Private.
3. John,	Hadley,	Private.
4. John,	Hingham,	Private.
5. John,	Marlborough,	Private.
6. Joseph,	Hadley,	Private.
7. Joseph,	Oxford,	Private.
8. Joseph,	Westfield,	Private.
9. Nathaniel,	Hatfield,	Private.
10. Thomas,	Groton,	Private.
11. Thomas,	not given,	Private.
12. Thomas,	not given,	Private.
13. Richard,	Northfield,	Private.
14. William,	Billerica,	Private.
15. William,	Hull,	Private.

Members of the Chamberlain family in Massachusetts who served in the Revolution:†

Christian Name.	Place of Enlistment.	Rank.
1. Abel,	Chelmsford,	Private.
2. Abel,	Chelmsford,	Private.
3. Abraham,	Hardwick,	Sergeant.

*Ephraim Chamberlain, of Northfield, served as a private at Louisburg under Pepperell. Theophilus Chamberlain, of Northfield, served as a private in Burke's Rangers at the capture of Fort William Henry by Montcalm.

† Ephraim, of Northfield, was a captain in the army, and his brother Samuel was a major.

Christian Name.	Place of Enlistment.	Rank.
4. Amasa,	Sutton,	Matross.
5. Aaron,	Falmouth,	Private.
6. Ashael,	Worcester Co.,	Private.
7. Benjamin,	Chelmsford,	Private.
8. Benjamin,	Chelmsford,	Sergeant.
9. Benjamin,	Leicester,	Sergeant.
10. Benjamin,	Pepperell,	Private.
11. Benjamin,	Winchendon,	Private.
12. Benjamin,	Winchester,	Private.
13. Benjamin,	Becket,	First Lieutenant.
14. Benjamin,	Hardwick,	Private.
15. Benjamin,	Boston,	First Lieutenant.
16. Benjamin,	not given,	Private.
17. Abel,	Boston,	Private.
18. Aaron,	Chelmsford,	Private.
19. Benjamin,	Bridgewater,	Private.
20. Benjamin,	Chelmsford,	Fifer.
21. Benjamin,	Spencertown,	Private.
22. Benjamin,	Sutton,	Private.
23. Daniel,	Westborough,	Private.
24. David,	Hardwick,	Private.
25. David,	Brookfield,	Drummer.
26. David,	Pepperell,	Private.
27. David,	Spencer,	Private.
28. David,	not given,	Private.
29. David,	not given,	Private.
30. Ebenezer,	Charlton,	Private.
31. Ebenezer,	Westborough,	Sergeant.
32. Ebenezer,	Westborough,	Private.
33. Edmund,	Southborough,	Sergeant.

	Christian Name.	Place of Enlistment.	Rank.
34.	Elisha,	Berkshire Co.,	Private.
35.	Enoch,	Holliston,	Private.
36.	Ephraim,	Westford,	Private.
37.	Freedom,	Pembroke,	Captain.
38.	Garland,	Lynn,	Private.
39.	Daniel,	Westford,	Private.
40.	Ebenezer,	Boston,	Sergeant.
41.	Edmund,	Southborough,	Second Lieutenant.
42.	Edmund,	not given,	F'st Lieut. Marines.
43.	Eliakim,	not given,	Private.
44.	Elisha,	not given,	Private.
45.	Elisha,	Berkshire Co.,	Private.
46.	Elisha,	not given,	Private.
47.	Ephraim,	Bolton,	Private.
48.	Ephraim,	Yarmouth,	Private.
49.	Ichabod,	Dudley,	Private.
50.	Isaac,	Chelmsford,	Private.
51.	Job,	Abington,	Private.
52.	Jacob,	Dudley,	Corporal.
53.	Jacob,	Hopkinton,	Private.
54.	James,	not given,	Private.
55.	Jason,	Concord,	Private.
56.	Job,	not given,	Private.
57.	John,	Marshfield,	Private.
58.	John,	Pepperell,	Private.
59.	John,	Suffolk,	Private.
60.	John,	Sutton,	Private.
61.	Jacob,	not given,	Sergeant.
62.	Jason,	not given,	Sergeant.
63.	Joel,	not given,	Private.

Christian Name.	Place of Enlistment.	Rank.
64. John,	Ashburnham,	Private.
65. John,	Fitzwilliam,	Private.
66. John,	Douglas,	Private.
67. John,	Westford,	Private.
68. John,	Worcester,	Private.
69. John,	not given,	Private.
70. John,	not given,	Private.
71. John,	not given,	Private.
72. John,	not given,	Private.
73. John,	Plympton,	Corporal.
74. Joseph,	Middleboro'.	Private.
75. Joseph,	Westborough,	Private.
76. Joseph,	Plymouth Co.,	Private.
77. Joseph,	Charlton,	Private.
78. Joseph,	Pepperell,	Private.
79. Joseph,	Pittsfield,	Sergeant.
80. Joseph,	Plympton,	Private.
81. Joseph,	Kingston,	Private,
82. Joseph,	Roxbury,	Private.
83. Joseph,	Georgetown,	Private.
84. Joseph,	Berkshire Co.,	Private.
85. Joseph,	not given,	Private.
86. Joseph,	not given,	Private.
87. Joseph,	not given,	Fifer.
88. Joshua,	Balltown,	Private.
89. Joshua,	Richmond,	Private.
90. Joshua,	Westborough,	Corporal.
91. Joshua,	Pannelborough,	Private.
92. Joshua,	Westborough,	Sergeant.
93. Joshua,	not given,	Private.

Christian Name.	Place of Enlistment.	Rank.
94. Josiah,	New Marlboro',	Private.
95. Josiah,	Worcester,	Private.
96. Josiah,	Plymouth,	Corporal.
97. Josiah,	not given,	Private.
98. Lemuel,	Boston or Roxbury,	Private.
99. Lewis,	not given,	Private.
100. Lewis,	Bridgewater,	Private.
101. Lemuel,	Southborough,	Private.
102. Moses,	Hardwick,	Private.
103. Moses,	Pepperell,	Private.
104. Moses,	Walpole,	Private.
105. Moses,	not given,	Private.
106. Nathaniel,	Hopkinton,	Private.
107. Nathaniel,	Needham,	Private.
108. Nathaniel,	Westford,	Private.
109. Nathaniel,	Westborough,	Fifer.
110. Nathaniel,	not given,	Sergeant.
111. Nathaniel,	not given,	Sergeant-Major.
112. Nathaniel,	not given,	Private.
113. Nathaniel,	Pembroke,	Corporal.
114. Nathaniel,	· not given,	Private.
115. Nathaniel,	not given,	Private.
116. Phineas,	Hopkinton,	Private.
117. Richard,	Boston,	Private.
118. Richard,	Great Barrington,	Private.
119. Russell,	Great Barrington,	Private.
120. Samuel,	Chelmsford,	Private.
121. Samuel,	Richmond,	Private.
122. Samuel,	Sandisfield,	Private.
123. Samuel,	not given,	Private.

Christian Name.	Place of Enlistment.	Rank.
124. Samuel,	not given,	Private.
125. Simon,	Newton,	Private.
126. Silas,	Dracut,	Private.
127. Silas,	Billerica,	Private.
128. Staples,	Hollister,	Captain.
129. Staples,	Roxbury,	Second Lieutenant.
130. Thomas,	Harvard,	Private.
131. Thomas,	Squantum,	Private.
132. Thomas,	Royalston,	Sergeant.
133. Thomas,	Boston,	First Lieutenant.
134. Thomas,	not given,	Sergeant.
135. Thomas,	Plymouth,	Private.
136. Timothy,	Sturbridge,	Private.
137. Wilder,	Hollis,	Private.
138. William,	Andover,	Private.
139. William,	Hardwick,	Private.
140. William,	Hatfield,	Corporal.
141. William,	Scarborough,	Private.
142. William,	Wilmington,	Private.
143. William,	not given,	Seaman, Brigantine Massachusetts.
144. William,	not given,	Private.
145. William,	not given,	Private.
146. William,	not given,	Private.
147. William,	York Co.,	Private.
148. William,	Greenwich,	Private.
149. William,	Plymouth Co.,	Private.
150. Wilson,	Worcester,	Private.
151. William,	Biddeford,	Private.
152. Wilson,	Bennington,	Private.

Members of the Chamberlain family in Connecticut who served in the Colonial Wars:

Christian Name.	Place of Residence or Reg't.	Rank.
1. Benjamin,	Colchester,	Lieutenant.
2. Benjamin,	Colchester,	Ensign.
3. Daniel,	Colchester,	Lieutenant.
4. John,	12th Regiment,	Quartermaster.
5. John,	11th Regiment,	Lieutenant.
6. John,	12th Regiment,	Captain.
7. John,	Havana Expedition,	Ensign.
8. Joseph,	Hartford Co.,	Quartermaster.
9. Nathaniel,	not given,	Quartermaster.
10. Nathaniel, Jr.,	not given,	Cornet.

Members of the Chamberlain family in Connecticut who served in the Revolution:

Christian Name.	Rank.
1. Aaron,	Private.
2. Abiel,	Clerk.
3. Bartlett,	Fifer.
4. Benjamin,	Private.
5. Daniel,	Private.
6. Edmond,	Sergeant.
7. Eleazer,	Sergeant.
8. Eliphalet,	First Lieutenant.
9. Ephraim,	Captain.
10. Ephraim,	Private.
11. Isaac,	Private.
12. Elisha,	Private.
13. Green,	Private.

Christian Name.		Rank.
14.	Jeremiah,	Private.
15.	Joel,	Second Lieutenant.
16.	Joel,	Ensign.
17.	John,	Ensign.
18.	Joseph,	Corporal.
19.	Joseph H.,	Private.
20.	Leander,	Private.
21.	Luther,	Private.
22.	Oliver,	Private.
23.	Peleg,	Sergeant.
24.	Plinn,	Private.
25.	Richard,	Private.
26.	Samuel,	Private.
27.	Stephen,	Private.
28.	Swift,	Private.
29.	Theodore,	Private.
30.	Waitt,	Private.
31.	William,	Private.

Members of the Chamberlain family in New York who served in the Colonial Wars:

Christian Name.		Residence.	Rank.
1.	Benjamin,	Queens Co.,	Private.
2.	Isaac,	Albany,	Private.
3.	Jonathan,	Claverack,	Private.
4.	Philip,	Claverack,	Private.

Members of the Chamberlain family in New York who served in the Revolutionary War:

Christian Name.		Rank.
1.	Amos,	Lieutenant.
2.	Colby,	Captain.
3.	John,	Sergeant.
4.	John,	Lieutenant.
5.	William,	Lieutenant.
6.	Benjamin,	Private.
7.	Gordon or Girdon,	Private.
8.	Jehu,	Private.
9.	Jacob,	Private.
10.	Joseph,	Private.
11.	Judah,	Private.
12.	Wyatt,	Private.

Members of the Chamberlain family in New Jersey who served in the Revolution:

CONTINENTAL TROOPS.

Christian Name.		Rank.
1.	Lewis,	Private.
2.	David,	Private.
3.	Seth,	Private.
4.	Uriah,	Private.

NEW JERSEY MILITIA.

Christian Name.		Residence.	Rank.
5.	Aaron,	Monmouth,	Private.
6.	Clayton,	Hunterdon,	Private.
7.	David,	Hunterdon,	Private.

Christian Name.	Residence.	Rank.
8. Godfrey,	Hunterdon,	Private.
9. Henry,	Monmouth,	Private.
10. James,	Sussex,	Private.
11. John,	Hunterdon,	Private.
12. John,	Sussex,	Private.
13. John,	Middlesex,	Private.
14. Joseph,	Middlesex,	Private.
15. Lewis,	Middlesex,	Private.
16. Lewis,	Hunterdon,	Private.
17. Seth,	Hunterdon,	Private.
18. Thomas,	Gloucester,	Private.
19. Thomas,	Middlesex,	Private.
20. William,	Hunterdon,	Lieut.-Colonel.
21. William,	Hunterdon,	Private.
22. Zephaniah,	Sussex,	Private.
23. Niean,	not given,	Wagonmaster.

MARYLAND.

James Chamberlaine, Brigadier-General, Maryland Militia, 1776.

NOTE.— The Committee will be pleased to receive notification of any omissions or errors in these lists.— *Editor.*

LIST OF THE REVOLUTIONARY PENSION CLAIMS FILED FROM NEW ENGLAND STATES IN THE NAME OF CHAMBERLAIN OR CHAMBERLIN.

Nathaniel	Invalid File No. 18	778
John	19	241
Benjamin	21	687
Ephraim	28	679
Pliney	29	708
Joshua	34	687
Aaron	36	963
Moses	36	967
Ebenezer	39	300
Joseph	39	303
Benjamin	39	306
David	44	727
Benjamin	44	734
Samuel	44	735
Benjamin	Widow File No. 23	792
Josiah	17	608
Russell	16	896
Nathaniel	15	963
Thomas	14	475
John	14	461
Lewis	8	604
Phineas	1	716

New Hampshire.

Henry	Invalid File No. 38	601
Ebenezer	39	299
Calvin	39	310
Daniel	44	384
James	45	626
Jason	45	627
Elisha	46	876
Moses	Widow File No. 4	652
Thomas	22	767
Ephraim	25	060
Elias	25	413
Elisha	Rejected 1	835

Vermont.

Charles	Invalid File No. 23	154
Joel	Widow File No. 16	903
John	25	402
Elias	25	413

Maine.

Silas	Widow File No. 23	788

Connecticut.

Iireh	Invalid File No. 22	170
Joseph S.	37	841
Samuel	37	826
Leander	40	826
William	44	733
Isaac	45	836

Swift	.	.	.			Widow File No.		1	555
Theodore	.	.	.	.	.	.	.	1	226
Nathaniel	.	.	.	.	.	.	.	14	474
Jeremiah	.	.		.	.	.	.	23	790
Aaron	.	.	.	.	.	.	.	27	394

NOTE.— The above list was presented to the Association, September 19, 1900, by Dr. William R. Chamberlain, Washington, D. C. It was taken from the original files.—*Editor*.

TREASURER'S REPORT.

Thomas Chamberlain,
In Account with The Chamberlain Association.

To amount received from the Asst. Treasurer, $50.00
October, 1898, . . .	$25.00
October, 1899, . . .	25.00

Boston, September 19, 1900.

Mrs. Sophia A. C. Caswell,
In Account with The Chamberlain Association.

1899.	Dr.				
Aug. 30.	Balance on hand, .	.	.	.	$115.91
	Membership fees,	.	.	.	224.00
	One Life Member,	.	.	.	25.00
	Sales of Reports,	.	.	.	5.05
					$369.96

	Cr.			
Oct.	Paid Treasurer, .	.	$25.00	
	Banquet, .	.	16.50	
	Printing, .	.	154.83	
	Stationery and stamps,		33.06	229.39
	Balance on hand,	.	.	$140.57

SPECIAL FUND, DONATED FOR ADMINISTRATION OF THE
GENEALOGICAL BUREAU.

DR.

Rev. Dr. L. T. Chamberlain, . . .	$100.00
Hon. D. H. Chamberlain, ...	100.00
Mr. Jacob Chester Chamberlain, . .	100.00
	$300.00

CR.

Paid to Chairman Genealogical Committee, .	$300.00

SUMMARY.

Cash in hands of Treasurer, ...	$50.00
" " " " Asst. Treasurer, . .	140.57
Total cash on hand, ...	$190.57

OFFICERS FOR THE CURRENT YEAR.

President.
MAJ.-GEN. JOSHUA L. CHAMBERLAIN, LL. D., Brunswick, Me.

Vice-Presidents.
HON. DANIEL H. CHAMBERLAIN, LL. D., West Brookfield, Mass.
BRIG.-GEN. SAMUEL E. CHAMBERLAIN, Barre, Mass.
COL. THOMAS CHAMBERLIN, Philadelphia, Pa.
REV. E. E. STRONG, D. D., Boston, Mass.
PROF. T. C. CHAMBERLIN, LL. D., Chicago, Ill.
MYRON L. CHAMBERLAIN, M. D., Boston, Mass.
COL. SIMON E. CHAMBERLIN, Washington, D. C.
COL. HENRY H. ADAMS, New York.
MR. L. H. CHAMBERLIN, Detroit, Mich.
PRES. MCKENDREE H. CHAMBERLAIN, LL. D., Lebanon, Ill.
CAPT. A. P. ANDREW, La Porte, Ind.

Corresponding Secretary.
MISS ABBIE M. CHAMBERLAIN, Washington, D. C., and
Box 218, Braintree, Mass.

Recording Secretary.
MR. ASA W. CHAMBERLIN, Jamaica Plain, Mass.

Treasurer.
MR. THOMAS CHAMBERLAIN, State National Bank, Boston.

Assistant Treasurer.
MRS. SOPHIA A. CHAMBERLAIN CASWELL, 27 River Street,
Cambridgeport, Mass.

Additional Members of Executive Committee.
MISS LAURA B. CHAMBERLAIN, Washington, D. C.
MR. MONTAGUE CHAMBERLAIN, Cambridge, Mass.
MR. THOMAS E. CHAMBERLIN, Brookline, Mass.

STANDING COMMITTEES.

Genealogical Committee.

MR. JACOB CHESTER CHAMBERLAIN, *Chairman*, 1 W. 81st Street, New York.

COL. THOMAS CHAMBERLIN, Philadelphia, Pa.

MR. HERBERT B. CHAMBERLAIN, Brattleboro, Vt.

G. M. CHAMBERLIN, M. D., Chicago, Ill.

MISS JENNIE CHAMBERLAIN WATTS, Cambridge, Mass.

JOSEPH E. N. CHAMBERLAIN, M. D., Easton, Md.

REV. L. T. CHAMBERLAIN, D. D., New York.

Committee on Colonial and American Revolutionary History.

J. W. CHAMBERLIN, M. D., *Chairman*, Endicott Building, St. Paul, Minn.

MR. WILLIAM S. BOYNTON, St. Johnsbury, Vt.

MRS. H. H. BURNHAM, Putnam, Conn.

PROF. PAUL MELLEN CHAMBERLAIN, Chicago, Ill.

MRS. O. A. FURST, Bellefonte, Pa.

MISS S. EMMA CHAMBERLIN, Cleveland, O.

MR. PRESCOTT CHAMBERLAIN, Boston, Mass.

Committee on English Ancestry.

REV. L. T. CHAMBERLAIN, D. D., *Chairman*, The Chelsea, New York.

MR. JOHN WILSON CHAMBERLIN, Tiffin, O.

MRS. HARRIET P. KIMBALL, Dubuque, Iowa.

MR. JOHN C. ORDWAY, Concord, N. H.

MR. HENRY R. CHAMBERLAIN, London, England.

LIST OF MEMBERS.

(Those in heavy-faced type are "charter" members; those marked with an asterisk are dead.)

ACTIVE MEMBERS.

Col. HENRY H. ADAMS,	New York, N. Y.
Capt. A. P. ANDREW,	La Porte, Ind.
— Mrs. MARTHA E. AUSTIN,	Roxbury, Mass.
Mrs. E. S. BARTLETT,	Evanston, Ill.
— **Mrs. Ellen E. C. Blair,**	Dorchester, Mass.
Miss AMY E. BLANCHARD,	Philadelphia, Pa.
*Mr. D. C. BLOOMER,	Council Bluffs, Iowa.

(Died February 26, 1900.)

Mrs. S. M. BODWELL,	Clifton Springs, N. Y.
Mr. William S. Boynton,	St. Johnsbury, Vt.
Mrs. J. M. Brant,	East Weymouth, Mass.
Mrs. GEORGE M. BROWN,	Hartford, Conn.
Mrs. J. S. BROWNE,	La Grange, Ind.
Mrs. Mary C. Burnham,	Putnam, Conn.
Mrs. CARRIE M. BUTTS,	Newton Centre, Mass.
Mrs. EMILY A. CAPRON,	Winchendon, Mass.
Mrs. Sophia A. C. Caswell,	Cambridgeport, Mass.
Miss Abbie M. Chamberlain,	Washington, D. C.
Mr. A. C. Allen Chamberlain,	Winchester, Mass.
Miss ALICE CHAMBERLAIN,	Hyde Park, Mass.
Mr. ALLEN CHAMBERLIN,	New York, N. Y.
ALLEN H. CHAMBERLAIN, M. D.,	Foxcroft, Me.

Miss ANNA P. CHAMBERLAIN,	East Orange, N. J.
Mr. ANSEL E. CHAMBERLIN,	Dalton, Mass.
Mr. ARTHUR B. CHAMBERLAIN,	Rochester, N. Y.
Miss A. S. CHAMBERLIN,	Hartford, Conn.
Mr. Asa W. Chamberlin,	Jamaica Plain, Mass.
Mr. BURR C. CHAMBERLIN,	Dalton, Mass.
Miss CATHARINE J. CHAMBERLAYNE,	Boston, Mass.—
Mr. CECIL C. CHAMBERLAIN,	Enderlin, North Dakota.
Mr. CHARLES A. CHAMBERLIN,	Detroit, Mich.
Mr. CHARLES A. CHAMBERLIN,	Westford, Mass.
Mr. CHARLES E. CHAMBERLIN,	Roxbury, Mass.
Mr. CHARLES H. CHAMBERLIN,	Dalton, Mass.
Mr. CHARLES H. CHAMBERLIN,	Kingston, Pa.
*Mr. CHARLES K. CHAMBERLIN,	Pittsburg, Pa.

(Died May 14, 1899.)

Mr. CHARLES T. CHAMBERLAIN,	Minneapolis, Minn.
Mr. CLARK W. CHAMBERLAIN,	La Grange, Ohio.
***Cyrus N. Chamberlain, M. D.,**	Andover, Mass.

(Died July 18, 1899.)

Mr. CHARLES W. CHAMBERLAIN,	Dayton, Ohio.
Mr. CHAUNCY W. CHAMBERLAIN,	Boston, Mass. —
Mr. CLARENCE M. CHAMBERLAIN,	Rochester, N. Y.
Hon. Daniel H. Chamberlain, LL. D.,	
	West Brookfield, Mass.
***Hon. Daniel U. Chamberlin,**	Cambridgeport, Mass.

(Died June 15, 1898.)

Miss DELIA CARA CHAMBERLIN,	Burlington, Iowa.
Mr. DWIGHT S. CHAMBERLAIN,	Lyons, N. Y.
Mr. EDWARD WILLMOT CHAMBERLAIN,	New York, N. Y.
Mr. Edward Watts Chamberlain,	Louisville, Ky.
Mr. EDWIN A. CHAMBERLIN,	Trenton, N. J.

65

Edwin C. Chamberlin, M. D.,	New York, N. Y.
Miss Elisabeth Chamberlin,	Torresdale, Pa.
Miss Elisabeth E. Chamberlain,	Providence, R. I.
Miss Ella J. Chamberlain,	Cambridge, Mass.
Mr. Ephraim Chamberlain,	Medfield, Mass.
Mr. Ernest V. Chamberlin,	Cincinnati, Ohio.
Mr. Eugene G. Chamberlin,	Chicago, Ill.
Mr. Eugene Tyler Chamberlain,	Washington, D. C.
Gen. Frank Chamberlain,	Albany, N. Y.
Mr. Frank D. Chamberlain,	Columbus, Ohio.
Mr. Frank E. Chamberlain,	Manistee, Mich.
Mr. Frank H. Chamberlain,	Hudson, Mass.
Mr. Frederic E. Chamberlin,	Bayonne, N. J.
Mr. Fred W. Chamberlin,	Detroit, Mich.
Miss F. D. Chamberlin,	Hartford, Conn.
Mr. F. W. Chamberlain,	Three Oaks, Mich.
Mr. George B. Chamberlin,	Chicago, Ill.
Mr. George F. Chamberlin,	New York, N. Y.
Mr. G. Howard Chamberlin,	Yonkers, N. Y.
Mr. George M. Chamberlin, M. D.,	Chicago, Ill.
Mr. George R. Chamberlain,	New Haven, Conn.
Rev. George W. Chamberlain,	Bahia, Brazil, S. A.
Mr. George W. Chamberlain,	Weymouth, Mass.
Mr. G. T. Chamberlain,	Columbus, Ohio.
Miss Gertrude Chamberlin,	Boston, Mass.
Mr. Harlow H. Chamberlain,	Minneapolis, Minn.
Mr. Harry G. Chamberlin,	Chicago, Ill.
Miss Helen Chamberlain,	Hyde Park, Mass.
Miss Henrietta M. Chamberlaine,	Baltimore, Md.
Mr. Henry Chamberlain,	Three Oaks, Mich.

66

Mr. HENRY E. CHAMBERLIN,	Gridley, Kan.
Mr. HENRY R. CHAMBERLAIN,	London, England.
Mr. Herbert B. Chamberlin,	Brattleboro, Vt.
Mr. HIRAM S. CHAMBERLAIN,	Chattanooga, Tenn.
Mr. HORACE P. CHAMBERLAIN,	Buffalo, N. Y.
Mr. I. C. CHAMBERLAIN,	Dubuque, Iowa.
Miss ISABELLA S. CHAMBERLIN,	Washington, D. C.
Rev. JACOB CHAMBERLAIN, D. D.,	Madanapalle, India.
Mr. JACOB A. CHAMBERLAIN,	Warwick, N. Y.
Mr. Jacob Chester Chamberlain,	New York, N. Y.
Rev. JAMES A. CHAMBERLIN,	Torrington, Conn.
Mr. JAMES F. CHAMBERLAIN,	Los Angeles, Cal.
Mr. JAMES ROSWELL CHAMBERLIN,	Rochester, N. Y.
Mr. JAMES W. CHAMBERLAIN,	Akron, Ohio.
Miss Jessie C. Chamberlin,	Boston, Mass.
Mr. JOHN C. CHAMBERLIN,	Dalton, Mass.
Mr. JOHN F. CHAMBERLIN,	Summit, N. J.
Mr. JOHN WILSON CHAMBERLIN,	Tiffin, Ohio.
JOSEPH E. N. CHAMBERLAIN, M. D.,	Easton, Md.
Maj.-Gen. Joshua L. Chamberlain, LL. D.,	
	Brunswick, Me.
Mr. J. D. CHAMBERLIN,	Toledo, Ohio.
Mr. J. H. CHAMBERLIN,	Chicago, Ill.
J. P. CHAMBERLIN, M. D.,	Boston, Mass.
Mr. J. R. CHAMBERLAIN,	Raleigh, N. C.
J. W. Chamberlin, M. D.,	St. Paul, Minn.
Miss Laura B. Chamberlain,	Cambridge, Mass.
Mr. LEON T. CHAMBERLAIN,	St. Paul, Minn.
Mr. LEWIS H. CHAMBERLIN,	Detroit, Mich.
Miss Lizzie F. Chamberlain,	Cambridge, Mass

Mark A. Chamberlain, M. D.,   Winthrop, Iowa.
Mr. Martin H. Chamberlin,   Rutland, Vt.
Miss Mary Chamberlin,   Torresdale, Pa.
— Miss Mary Dunton Chamberlain,   Roxbury, Mass.
Pres. McKendree H. Chamberlin, LL. D.,

    Lebanon, Ill.
*Hon. Mellen Chamberlain, LL. D.,   Chelsea, Mass.
    (Died June 25, 1900.)
— Mr. Montague Chamberlain,   Cambridge, Mass.
·— Myron L. Chamberlain, M. D.,   Boston, Mass.
·· Mr. Nahum B. Chamberlain,   Jamaica Plain, Mass.
Mr. Newell Chamberlain,   Cambridge, Mass.
Mr. Norman A. Chamberlain,   Charleston, S. C.
*Miss N. Augusta Chamberlain,   Auburndale, Mass.
    (Died March 22, 1900.)
Rev. N. H. Chamberlayne,   Monument Beach, Mass.
Mr. Oren S. Chamberlain,   Chicago, Ill.
Capt. Orville T. Chamberlain,   Elkhart, Ind.
Mr. Patrick Chamberlaine,   Chicago, Ill.
Prof. Paul Mellen Chamberlain,   Chicago, Ill.
Mr. Prescott Chamberlain,   Chelsea, Mass.
Miss Phœbanna Chamberlain,   Orange, N. J.
Mr. Richard H. Chamberlain,   Oakland, Cal.
Gen. Robert H. Chamberlain,   Worcester, Mass.
Mr. Rollin S. Chamberlin,   Wilkesbarre, Pa.
Mr. Roswell W. Chamberlain,   Chester, N. Y.
Brig.-Gen. Samuel E. Chamberlain,

    Barre Plain, Mass.
Miss Sarah P. Chamberlain,   Salem, Mass.
Mr. Simeon E. Chamberlain,   Kansas City, Mo.

Col. Simon E. Chamberlin,	Washington, D. C.
Mrs. SARAH C. E. CHAMBERLIN,	Buenos Ayres, S. A.
Miss S. Emma Chamberlin,	Cleveland, Ohio.
Miss S. D. CHAMBERLIN,	Hartford, Conn.
Mr. S. S. CHAMBERLAIN,	Chicago, Ill.
Mr. S. T. CHAMBERLIN,	Derby, Conn.
Mr. STILLMAN W. CHAMBERLIN,	Braintree, Mass.
Prof. T. C. Chamberlin, LL. D.,	Chicago, Ill.
Col. Thomas Chamberlin,	Philadelphia, Pa.
Mr. Thomas Chamberlain,	Hyde Park, Mass.
Mr. THOMAS F. CHAMBERLIN,	Brookline, Mass.
Mr. WARD B. CHAMBERLIN,	New York, N. Y.
Mr. WARREN CHAMBERLAIN,	Honolulu, H. I.
Mr. WILBUR F. CHAMBERLAIN,	Hannibal, Mo.
Mr. WILLARD DeWITT CHAMBERLIN,	Dayton, Ohio.
Mr. WILLARD N. CHAMBERLAIN,	Watertown, Mass.
Mr. WILLIAM CHAMBERLAIN,	Portland, Me.
Prof. WILLIAM B. CHAMBERLAIN,	Oak Park, Ill.
Mr. WILLIAM B. CHAMBERLIN,	Torresdale, Pa.
Mr. WILLIAM C. CHAMBERLAIN,	Charlottesville, Va.
Mr. WILLIAM C. CHAMBERLAIN,	Dubuque, Iowa.
Mr. William Carlton Chamberlain,	Louisville, Ky.
Mr. WILLIAM H. CHAMBERLIN,	Chicago, Ill.
Mr. WILLIAM H. CHAMBERLIN,	Cincinnati, Ohio.
Mr. WILLIAM H. CHAMBERLAIN,	Kanona, N. Y.
Mr. WILLIAM JOSEPH CHAMBERLAIN,	Denver, Col.
Mr. WILLIAM K. CHAMBERLIN,	Pittsfield, Mass.
Major WILLIAM N. CHAMBERLIN,	Washington, D. C.
Mr. WILLIAM PORTER CHAMBERLAIN,	Knoxville, Tenn.
Mr. WILLIAM S. CHAMBERLAIN,	Cleveland, Ohio.

Mrs. T. Eaton Clapp, Albany, N. Y.

Mr. Albert Chamberlain Clarke, Southbridge, Mass.

*Mrs. Alice G. Chamberlain Clarke,

Southbridge, Mass.

(Died July 8, 1899.)

Mrs. Mary L. C. Clarke, Andover, Mass.—

Mrs. Alfred W. Cole, Boston, Mass.—

Edward Cowles, M. D., Waverley, Mass. —

Mrs. Corydon Crain, Jamaica Plain, Mass. --

Mrs. T. W. Dale, Auburndale, Mass. --

Mrs. Amie Whiting Damon, Reading, Mass. -

Mrs. Nathan A. Davis, Concord, Mass. ·

Mrs. A. E. Dick, Andover, Mass.··

Mrs. Kate C. Dillingham, Denver, Col.

Mr. Charles N. Fessenden, Chicago, Ill.

Mr. Harriott A. Fox, Chicago, Ill.

Mrs. Caroline W. Furst, Bellefonte, Pa.

Miss M. E. Grover, White River Junction, Vt.

Mrs. Helen Guilford, Minneapolis, Minn.

Mrs. O. H. Harding, Allston, Mass. --

Mrs. Lucy Chamberlain Hayward, London, Eng.

Miss Louise H. Hinckley, Cambridge, Mass. --

Miss Lida Hooper, New York City, N. Y.

Mrs. H. T. C. Hughes, Mobile, Ala.

Mrs. Cleora E. Jefferds, Foxcroft, Me.

Miss Charlotte A. Jewell, Hartford, Conn.

Mrs. Annie B. Chamberlain Keene, Woodsford, Me.

Mrs. Etta F. C. Kendall, Auburndale, Mass.--

Mrs. Eliza M. C. Kennedy, Watertown, Mass. ·

Mr. Horace Kennedy, Watertown, Mass. ·

Mrs. Harriet P. Kimball, Dubuque, Iowa.

Mrs. HELEN M. C. LLOYD,	Chicago, Ill.
Mrs. C. B. McLEAN,	Pittsburg, Pa.
Mrs. JAMES A. MERRITT,	Baltimore, Md.
Mrs. FLORENCE CHAMBERLAIN MOSELY,	
	New Haven, Conn.
Mr. JOHN CHAMBERLAIN ORDWAY,	Concord, N. H.
Mrs. Carrie A. C. Oxford,	Eliot, Me.
Mr. George Herbert Perry,	Cambridge, Mass.
Mrs. Minnie A. C. Perry,	Cambridge, Mass.
Mr. Ralph Dana Perry,	Cambridge, Mass.
Mrs. CHARLES B. PLATT,	Englewood, N. J.
Mr. JOHN S. RINGWALT, Jr.,	Mt. Vernon, Ohio.
Mr. RALPH CURTIS RINGWALT,	Mt. Vernon, Ohio.
Mrs. ALBERT S. ROE,	New York, N. Y.
Miss EMMA TEN B. RUNK,	Lambertville, N. J.
Mrs. C. W. Seymour,	Hingham, Mass.
Mrs. ANNA EUGENIA SMILEY,	Marblehead, Mass.
Mr. ARTHUR C. SPRAGUE,	Wollaston, Mass.
Mr. FRANK H. SPRAGUE,	Wollaston, Mass.
Rev. E. E. Strong, D. D.,	Auburndale, Mass.
Miss Jennie Chamberlain Watts,	Cambridge, Mass.
Mrs. MARTHA C. WILSON,	Woodsford, Me.

ASSOCIATE MEMBERS.

Mr. GEORGE M. BROWN,	Hartford, Conn.
Mr. George B. Caswell,	Cambridgeport, Mass.
Mrs. ALICE RHEA CHAMBERLIN,	Torresdale, Pa.
Mrs. ANNA GARLAND CHAMBERLAIN,	Andover, Mass.
Mrs. Asa W. Chamberlin,	Jamaica Plain, Mass.
Mrs. EMMA B. CHAMBERLIN,	Chicago, Ill.
Mrs. EUGENE G. CHAMBERLIN,	Chicago, Ill.
Mrs. FANNIE E. CHAMBERLIN,	Philadelphia, Pa.
Mrs. JACOB C. CHAMBERLAIN,	New York, N. Y.
Mrs. M. A. CHAMBERLIN,	Greenville, N. H.
Mrs. Newell Chamberlain,	Cambridge, Mass.
Mrs. ROBERT H. CHAMBERLAIN,	Worcester, Mass.
Mrs. SAMUEL E. CHAMBERLAIN,	Barre Plain, Mass.
Mrs. CATHERINE W. CHAMBERLAIN,	Cambridge, Mass.
Mrs. THOMAS CHAMBERLAIN,	Hyde Park, Mass.
Mr. CHARLES DAMON,	Reading, Mass.
Mr. James H. Kendall,	Auburndale, Mass.
*Mr. Frank W. Perry,	Cambridge, Mass.
(Died June 20, 1898.)	
Mrs. WILLARD CHAMBERLAIN,	Watertown, Mass.

LIFE MEMBERS.

Mrs. LUCY P. CHAMBERLAIN,	Medford, Mass.
Rev. L. T. Chamberlain, LL. D.,	
	New York City, N. Y.

Chamberlain Association
of America.

*

ANNUAL REPORT.

1901

ABBIE MELLEN CHAMBERLAIN.

Chamberlain Association
of America
❧

REPORT OF ANNUAL MEETING

HELD IN BOSTON, MASSACHUSETTS

AUGUST, 1901

The Chamberlain Association of America.

ANNUAL MEETING OF 1901.

About fifty members responded to the call of the Executive Committee, and assembled at the Parker House, Boston, Wednesday, August 28th, 1901, at 10 o'clock, for their fourth annual business meeting and re-union. The two hours from ten to twelve were informally and delightfully spent in greetings and congratulations, as well as in forming the acquaintance of the members of the clan who were in attendance for the first time. The various committees also held sessions during this period.

The hour from twelve to one o'clock was devoted to a reception of the members by the President and those of the Vice-Presidents who were present; and at one o'clock the company, led by the President, General Joshua L. Chamberlain, and other officers, repaired to the "crystal" dining-room, where luncheon was served after grace had been said by Rev. E. E. Strong. The luncheon proved a pleasant innovation upon the evening banquet of former

3

gatherings, the company forming into small parties, and discussing such matters as were brought to their attention ; and the hearty responses heard above the hum of conversation evinced the scintillations of wit and humor characteristic of the family.

About half-past two, the President called the company to order, announcing that the time for the annual business meeting had arrived. After words of welcome, delivered in his usual graceful and characteristic manner, the records of the last annual meeting were called for, and were read by the Recording Secretary, and were approved.

The report of the Corresponding Secretary which is always listened to with great interest by the members, was read and accepted, and was put on file for publication in the Annual Report.

The financial report was presented by the Assistant Treasurer, and having been audited by the Executive Committee, was accepted.

The work of the Executive Committee during the year was reported by Mr. Montague Chamberlain. In this report, well deserved tributes were paid to the Corresponding Secretary and Assistant Treasurer, upon whom fall the burden of labor in conducting the affairs of the Association, and it was suggested that a portrait of the Corresponding Secretary, Miss Abbie M. Chamberlain, be inserted in the next Annual Report. The suggestion was enthusiastically applauded, and a vote was passed that the suggestion be carried out.

The reports of the Standing Committees were next in order, that of the Genealogical Committee being read by the Bureau Secretary. The report was accepted, and the Committee congratulated upon the work accomplished by them during the year. The report in full appears on another page.

The Committees on Colonial and Revolutionary History and on English Ancestry made no extended reports.

A vote was passed authorizing the President to appoint a Committee on Recent Wars, to compile a list of members of the family who took part in these wars.

On motion, the President appointed a committee to nominate officers for the ensuing year. The committee subsequently reported, recommending the re-election of the present board. The report was accepted and adopted, and the Recording Secretary was instructed to cast the vote of the Association for the nominees. This being done, the President declared these officers unanimously re-elected.

Gen. Samuel E. Chamberlain, of Barre, Mass., first Vice-President of the Association, made a brief speech, in which he suggested that the President should be furnished with a gavel for his use at

5

the meetings of the Association. He then referred
to the eminent services rendered by our President
during the Civil War, notably at the Battle of
Gettysburg, and thought that a gavel made of wood
from "Little Round Top" would be especially
fitting and of much historic value to the Association.
The suggestion was received with much enthusiasm
by the members, and a vote was passed instructing
the Executive Committee to procure the gavel.
Brief, but interesting speeches were also made by
Mr. Jacob C. Chamberlain, of New York, Dr.
Geo. M. Chamberlin, of Chicago, Ill., Mr. Thomas
Chamberlain, of Hyde Park, Mass., Mr. William
Chamberlain, of Portland, Me., Mr. Montague
Chamberlain, of Cambridge, Mass., and Milton
Reed, Esq., of Fall River, Mass., who was present
as the guest of Dr. Geo. M. Chamberlin.

The following greeting was received, and the
Corresponding Secretary was instructed to acknowledge the same :

August 15, 1901.

To the Chamberlain Association of America :

The descendants of Wright Chamberlain, Sr.,
now holding their tenth annual reunion in the hall
at Hop Bottom, Penn., send greetings and best

6

wishes to the CHAMBERLAIN ASSOCIATION OF AMERICA for Aug. 28, 1901.

(MISS) ENA BARBER,
Secretary.

MILTON, PA., August 1, 1901.

To the Officers and Members of the CHAMBERLAIN ASSOCIATION OF AMERICA, Boston, Mass.

Ladies and Gentlemen : — I feel very much gratified and highly honored by being enrolled as a member of your Association in which I have become interested through my daughter, Mrs. Furst, wife of Hon. A. O. Furst, of Bellefonte, Pennsylvania, who has been a member of your Association for several years past. It would afford me a great deal of pleasure to meet with you at your annual gathering, but the infirmities of age prevent me from being present, as I am now well up in my eighty-ninth year. I am in fair enjoyment of health in body and mind notwithstanding the infirmities of age.

I am the youngest child of William Chamberlin, late Lieutenant Colonel of a New Jersey Regiment of Volunteers during the Revolutionary War. Our family consisted of twenty-three children, the eldest of whom, my half-brother, Lewis Chamberlin, was

7

killed in the Battle of Germantown, the 4th day of October, 1777, aged eighteen years.

My father was one of the earliest settlers in this region, having moved to Buffalo Valley shortly after the Revolutionary War. He was a strong, resolute man, courageous and capable, and until the time of his death in 1817, was a recognized leader in his community, a trait which I have found characteristic of Chamberlins wherever found.

I have been a follower of John Wesley for seventy years past, and I am now patiently waiting the last summons to the better land.

I trust that your meeting will be a successful one ; that the Association will continue to increase in membership; that interest in it will never flag, and that the name Chamberlin will always be a symbol of power in the land.

With best wishes for you all I am,

Very sincerely yours,

MOSES CHAMBERLIN.

LEWIS INSTITUTE,
CHICAGO.

August 26, 1901.

To THE CHAMBERLAIN ASSOCIATION OF AMERICA.

Dear Friends: — I regret my inability to greet in person the members of this company assembled for the purpose of fraternal intercourse, and make

MOSES CHAMBERLIN.

acquaintances among you who are interested in the name which brings you together.

It has always been a pleasure to meet anyone bearing the name of Chamberlain and I have never had to record an instance of having to regret the possession of the name by the other person or by myself. I do not presume that everyone bearing the name is beyond reproach, but I mention my experience as a happy one.

" What's in a name? "

In the seven or eight generations in America preceding us, barring inter-marriages, we may find fifty-eight or one hundred and twenty-one direct ancestors bearing other family names than Chamberlain and while we are interested in such items of their personality as may be found, we are apt to expect more direct transmission of characteristics in the line bearing our name and in this connection nature gives us some startling examples of which I have one in mind :

Some years ago I saw a gentleman of whom I had no knowledge, whose resemblance to a relative of mine was so marked that I chanced addressing him as Mr. Chamberlain, and correctly. A pleasant acquaintanceship resulted and while we never were able to trace a common ancestor, we found that there were five generations intervening between the possibility of cousinship between the doubles.

But why do we desire to know of those men who were the carriers of our name? If we leave them alone, they are not likely to give us trouble. It has been said with irreverence that if one traces his line far enough, he is sure of finding a noose, but it has been with at least equal sagacity pointed out that one might profit by even such disagreeable discovery. It is not, however, the expectation of most people to discover disagreeables in their ancestral search, but if such be found, profit by them as well as by traits worthy of emulation.

In any undertaking it is wise to unearth, study, and analyze what has been previously done, then avoid the mistakes and profit by the successes. This is urged in the life of peoples, and how much more may it be urged for families. So far as I am informed, our early ancestors were not among the great men and it is equally noteworthy that few of the great men have headed families of continued greatness, but be that as it may, continued worth is preferable to anti-climaxes. If our forefathers were cobblers, let us hope they were conscientious ones; if soldiers, that they did not run when it was valorous to fight; if they were preachers, that they were true to their faith, and if they were day laborers, that they were such as command the respect of all honest people. If they were honest, intelligent, just people, as I have reason to believe most of them were, let us strive to allow no sag in the line to discourage future generations.

In addition to the pleasure of meeting annually, ought not this Association to commence the Chamberlain history, perhaps in magazine form, to stimulate interest and research which would in the course of time accumulate material suitable for the historian? The various committees, I presume, are collecting valuable material, but it does not reach and inspire as many as it might. The many family histories which have appeared in the last decade offer some examples of how not to proceed. A poorly constructed history is an unfortunate obstacle to increasing and sustained interest. Wishing a long life to the CHAMBERLAIN ASSOCIATION,

I am, yours truly,

PAUL MELLEN CHAMBERLAIN.

Letters of regret at inability to be present and greetings to the Association were received from

Hon. JOSEPH CHAMBERLAIN, Colonial Secretary, London, England.

Col. THOMAS CHAMBERLAIN, Philadelphia, Pa.

Pres. M. H. CHAMBERLAIN, Lebanon, Ill.

Col. H. H. ADAMS, New York City.

Mr. HERBERT B. CHAMBERLAIN, Brattleboro, Vt.

J. W. CHAMBERLAIN, M. D., St. Paul, Minn.

Mrs. O. A. FURST, Bellefonte, Pa.

Miss S. EMMA CHAMBERLAIN, Cleveland, Ohio.

Mr. PRESCOTT C. CHAMBERLAIN, Boston, Mass.

Mrs. H. P. KIMBALL, Dubuque, Iowa.

Miss AMY E. BLANCHARD, Philadelphia, Pa.

Mr. A. C. ALLEN CHAMBERLAIN, Winchester, Mass.

E. C. CHAMBERLAIN, M. D., N. Y. City.

Mr. ERNEST V. CHAMBERLAIN, Cincinnati, Ohio.

Com. EUGENE S. & Mrs. CHAMBERLAIN, Washington, D. C.

Miss GERTRUDE CHAMBERLAIN, Oxford, England.

Miss HENRIETTA MARIA CHAMBERLAIN, Baltimore, Md.

MARK A. CHAMBERLAIN, M. D., Winthrop, Iowa.

Capt. ORVILLE S. CHAMBERLAIN, Elkhart, Ind.

Mr. RICHARD H. CHAMBERLAIN, Oakland, California.

Miss SARAH P. CHAMBERLAIN, Salem, Mass.

Miss S. EMMA CHAMBERLAIN, Cleveland, Ohio.

Mrs. S. EATON CLAPP, Brooklyn, N. Y.

Dr. EDWARD COWLES, Waverley, Mass.

Miss H. A. FOX, Chicago, Ill.

Miss CHARLOTTE A. JEWELL, Hartford, Conn.

Mrs. LUCY P. CHAMBERLAIN, Windsor, Vt.

Mr. WILLIAM CHAMBERLAIN, West Chesterfield, N. H.

Mr. O. H. LELAND, Springfield, Vt.

Miss ENA BARBER, Saxonville, Pa.

Gen. ROBERT CHAMBERLAIN, Worcester, Mass.

Senator LOYED E. CHAMBERLAIN, Brockton, Mass.

Mr. & Mrs. W. P. CHAMBERLAIN, Knoxville, Penn.

Miss E. S. B. RUNK, Lambertville, N. J.
Mr. J. E. CHAMBERLAIN, New York.

During the luncheon, the Company were favored with several songs by Mrs. Herbert A. Austin, of Roxbury, Mass., and piano selections by Miss Anna P. Chamberlain, of East Orange, N. J., and Mrs. W. G. Newell, of Hingham, Mass.

The President appointed the following committee to nominate candidates for the offices of the Association at next year's General Meeting: Jacob Chester Chamberlain, Thomas E. Chamberlin, Frank H. Chamberlain.

The meeting adjourned at 5 o'clock.

REPORT OF THE CORRESPONDING SECRETARY.

Our Society has passed the experimental stage, for we find at the close of our fourth Annual Meeting, that we have since its formation enrolled 250 names upon our register. Hereafter we shall depend largely upon the co-operation of our own members to maintain the interest and increase the numbers of this Society.

The work for the past year has been pleasant work and it has been a progressive year in some respects. Our effort has been to broaden the interest in certain departments, and a healthy activity generally prevails.

The key-note of this meeting is the interests of the Genealogical Bureau, which we seek to make a general family Repository of knowledge. Growth cannot always be tabulated, but in the calculus of forces a general sustained interest must accompany an increase of members. Members of this Society, like Mr. Harrison in his first visit to America, have found something besides " mere bigness; " for this Association is composed of minds active in many fields of labor, members eminent as men of affairs, who see the trend and feel the needs of the age, yet are desirous to unite in one common purpose, to trace out family lives for posterity. This is an unselfish task with a noble aim.

But the food for hope is not found in our statistics, it is in the condition of the Society, which indicates a positive advance in several lines, as the reports will indicate. There is a satisfaction in feeling that we are no longer individual units, working with a strong individual note, but now have a kinship of purpose, which is an essay in the right direction : a means to an end — the brotherhood of a large family ! These reunions have brought about a better understanding, for all are working with one mind and will in a common cause for the general good.

It is said that a touch of kindred is a source of strength ; how much stronger and more intense it becomes when united in a Society ! The study of the lives of many ancestors is an incentive to strenuous noble living, and lends an interest to the sequence of events ; for we are often thrilled by what Emerson calls " the utterance of character."

Not all of the Chamberlains have a love of or a bump for Genealogy — some have not even passed through " the breakers of indifference," — hence there is an opportunity for our members to do considerable home missionary work. One of our

15

officers intimates that that must be a proof of our inheriting some of our French Tankerville blood; for the head of the ass on the coat of arms (of the Count of Tankerville) was not changed by some descendants to an eagle, until after their advent into England and the Norman blood was intermingled with the Saxon. The Eagle is the American national emblem, and naturally a responsive cord has been touched amongst the American Chamberlains, who would like to adopt it with its motto, *Spes et Fides*, Hope and Faith.

We have had a published Report from our Committee on the American Revolution and now there is a desire to have another Committee appointed for the later wars ; not to revive sectional feelings, for our Society " knows no North nor South," but they desire to complete a record of the men who were in the theatre of action in the recent history making epoch of our nation. Many of our family deserve a tablet in this Hall of Fame, for when the hour of opportunity occurred, the response and dynamic power were not lacking and no Rip Van Winkles were found amongst us.

The gathering last year was an interesting occasion, although at first saddened by the sudden illness and absence of our beloved President, but two of our Vice-Presidents, Brig.-Gen. S. E. Chamberlain and Dr. E. E. Strong, although indisposed themselves, rallied for the occasion and developed virile power under stress of circumstances. Their enthusiasm was contagious and their capital stories interspersed with brilliant music furnished by Miss Anna P. Chamberlain challenged every member to join in a general good social reunion. New officers were added and the whole constitutes a noble band, and with our committees we hope to press on the work of the Society.

Our faithful and loyal Mrs. Caswell is working to bring out a good surplus, to add to the permanent fund of the Society, while Mr. Montague Chamberlain has proved himself invaluable in editing the Annual Reports.

We would especially urge every member to aid or unite with our Genealogical Bureau in completing personal and family records. This Bureau was established to help all of the members to learn something of their ancestry, and it is the aim to do the work in an economical and satisfactory manner. If the members in a branch would unite to complete their records, it would simplify labor and expense. Will not the members take some action to encourage the energetic and generous Chairman, Mr. Jacob Chester Chamberlain?

We have prepared extracts from the letters of those who are not present, in order that you may make their acquaintance. We appreciate highly

their growing interest and encouraging words, and
hope that the Society will fulfil their highest expec-
tations.

Faithfully submitted,

ABBIE MELLEN CHAMBERLAIN,

Corresponding Secretary.

P. S. Last year, acting upon the suggestion of members of the
Executive Board, I made a more general report. in order to answer the
many letters of inquiry that had been received. — A. M. C.

NECROLOGY.

Since the last annual meeting the association has lost four members by death.

1900.
Dec. 30.   JOSEPH L. CHAMBERLAIN, Cherry Valley, New York.

1901.
Jan. 30.   JOSEPH E. M. CHAMBERLAINE, M.D., Easton, Md.

Apr. 1.   Rev. N. H. CHAMBERLAYNE, Monument Beach, Mass.

Aug. 9.   WILLIAM N. CHAMBERLAIN, Pittsfield, Mass.

Joseph Ennals Muse Chamberlaine was born at "Clora's Point" (his father's home) on Choptank River, Talbot County, eastern shore of Maryland, on February 18th, 1826. He studied medicine in Baltimore with Dr. Samuel Claggett Chew: graduated at the University of Maryland in 1850; practised medicine for one year in a Hospital in Baltimore, and for forty years in Easton. On January 14th, 1851, he married Elizabeth Bullitt Hayward, of Easton, who died in 1861, leaving two children, a son and daughter. On June 17th, 1866, Dr. Chamberlaine married S. Katherine Earle who died without children in October, 1900. Dr. Chamberlaine was an active member of the Protestant Episcopal Church and most highly esteemed and respected by the community at large, and his death was deeply deplored by his relatives and numerous friends.

The Chamberlaine family is one of the oldest of the English families who became represented in these States in early colonial days. During 800 years the Chamberlaines claimed by right four homesteads, two in England — Little Barrow and Saughall, in Cheshire — and two in America — Plain Dealing, on the Tred Avon, opposite Oxford, and Bonfield, on the Choptank, near Oxford. Bonfield, now the property of Dr. Chamberlaine, of Easton, is the only one of the four estates remaining in the family.

Richard Chamberlaine, Jr., was among the patentees of the first Virginia charter, in 1609, and with other merchant adventurers of the nobility, gentry, and artisans took stock in the commercial enterprises for opening North America. His son Thomas continued the trade his father had established. His sons, John and Samuel, born at Saughall, England, were the immigrants. John settled at Oxford and Samuel on the Plain Dealing estate. In 1721 he married Miss Mary Ungle, only child of Robert and Frances Ungle, and grand-daughter of John and Margaret Pope, who were among the earliest settlers of Oxford and owned large tracts of land on both sides of the Tred Avon river. She died in 1826, and three years after-ward he married Miss Henrietta Maria Lloyd, daughter of James and Ann Grundy Lloyd, of Wye House. All the Chamberlaines and their connections in this country trace back to this Samuel Chamberlaine, of Plain Dealing. Mr. Chamberlaine did not occupy this estate until after his second marriage, having then purchased it from the Ungle heirs. Mr. Chamberlaine, by his steady perseverance in commercial and agricultural pursuits soon became one of the richest men in the country, and owned thousands of acres of land on Tred Avon, Choptank, and Miles rivers. He stood among the first in the country as an honorable, honest and worthy man, proved by the high position he held for thirty-four years in the Lord Proprie-tary's Council of State. He died in 1773. The Chamberlaine family is connected with the Lloyds, Goldsboroughs, Robinses, Earles, DeCourseys, Tilghmans, Nicolses, Wrights, Hollydays, Gales, Kerrs, and Martins.

REPORT OF THE GENEALOGICAL COMMITTEE.

BOSTON, August 28, 1901.

The report of this Committee is really embodied in the report of the Genealogical Bureau. Our aim has been to develop its work along lines of greatest value to the Association itself, and also of personal interest to the greatest number of members.

We might, however, restate the purpose and work of this Bureau, set forth at its inauguration two years ago. As then stated the purpose of the Bureau's existence is to centralize and simplify researches in the Chamberlain genealogy, and so secure the highest efficiency in genealogical researches for the Association and for individual members desiring such information.

The Bureau Secretary's report gives the result of certain original researches, and shows what special investigations have been undertaken for individual members, eight out of ten having been brought to a successful issue within the year — an unusual accomplishment, and one for which our Secretary is greatly to be commended.

We can say little else than bespeak the continued use of the Bureau by members in tracing their ancestry, for so large an amount of Chamberlain data and information is now in our hands that the ancestry of many can be easily and inexpensively transcribed; excepting those cases which lead into problems similar to those given in the Bureau's report, and involving research of original and often very inaccessible records. The charge for all such work to members covers only the time and other contingent expenses involved.

The principal expenses in the maintenance of this Bureau have hitherto been and must continue to be met by generous contributions among our members; so this Committee will here make bold to encourage contributions toward the maintenance of the Bureau in its present activity, and if possible to enlarge and widen the field of its work.

THE GENEALOGICAL COMMITTEE.

REPORT OF THE GENEALOGICAL BUREAU.

The year has been one of fruitful growth. Our most valuable results have come from collections of unpublished vital statistics. The search has been broadened considerably this year.

The Bureau directed certain researches in Virginia for the purpose of ascertaining whether a Thomas Chamberlain and a William Chamberlain given in Hotten's "List of Emigrants" could be traced in Virginia from 1635 onward. Whoever searches in Virginia encounters greater difficulties than in searching in New England. The ravages of war destroyed the larger part of her early public records. We succeeded, however, in finding that there was a planter of the name William Chamberlain who lived in Charles City county and died there in 1661. The county records having been destroyed we secured abstracts to the name Chamberlain of all who received the Virginia land grants to 1770. We found no grants to any William Chamberlain, and the earliest one to a Thomas Chamberlain was made of land in Charles City county in 1690, when the Virginia immigrant of that name would be about seventy-five years of age.

GEORGE W. CHAMBERLAIN.

It is a matter of much doubt whether we have in these searches found any trace of that Thomas Chamberlain and of that William Chamberlain who sailed separately for Virginia in 1635. However, we did succeed in tracing the New Kent county family of Chamberlaynes through several generations, and have found good evidence that this branch, one of the most distinguished of the old families of Virginia, immigrated from the county of Hereford in England.

Considerable effort has been made to relate the New Jersey Chamberlins. The Bureau secured to that end a complete abstract of the probate records to the name from the entire State from 1667 to 1804. These, with the published documents, give us some good results, and it is fairly well established that the first of our name to settle in the East Jersey Colony about 1685, emigrated from Newport, Rhode Island, and were from ancestors of Quaker fame, but the relationship must yet be traced between the East Jersey families who settled in Monmouth county and the West Jersey families who appeared in Hunterdon county about fifty years after. To a dozen members of the Association this question is an exceedingly interesting and important one. Were Lewis Chamberlin, of Amwell, N. J., and his contemporary, Henry Chamberlin, of Hopewell, N. J., an adjoining

25

township, brothers and sons of some East Jersey Chamberlin whose name has not been associated in relationship? If not, who were the parents of these founders of large and honorable families?

Given time and persistence and I believe these questions can be satisfactorily answered.

In New England searches we have been more fortunate.

The descendants of the progenitor, William Chamberlain, and his wife, Rebecca, may congratulate themselves in being related to the most distinguished families of the Massachusetts Bay Colony. This discovery came by persistently following out a clew. The relationship appears in the will of a sister of Rebecca Chamberlain, whose fame had hitherto centered in the statement of James Savage that she died a witch in 1692. However much of truth the story of Rebecca, the witch, may contain, she certainly could lawfully claim people of note among her kinsfolk. Isaac Addington, Secretary of the Province of Massachusetts Bay for more than a quarter of a century, Chief Justice of the Superior Court of the Colony for two years, and Judge of Probate and Register for Suffolk county for the last fourteen years of his life, was her "kinsman." Rebecca Davenport, who was the mother of Addington Davenport, a graduate of Harvard College in 1689, and Judge of the Supreme

Court of the Colony for twenty-one years, was her "cousin." Colonel Penn Townsend, a Speaker of the House for several years, a member of His Majesty's Council for Massachusetts Bay, and at the time of his death Chief Judge of the Superior Court for Suffolk County, and his wife Sarah, were called "my cousins" in this will. It was Colonel Townsend's wife Sarah who was the mother of Penn Townsend, Jr., a graduate of Harvard in 1693, and of Sarah Townsend, who became the accomplished wife of the Rev. Ebenezer Thayer, for many years pastor of the Roxbury Church, where several families of our "kith and kin" then worshipped. Ann Pearce, who had formerly been the wife of Captain Samuel Moseley of Boston, that distinguished military commander in King Philip's War in 1675, was her "cousin;" while their daughter, Rebecca Moseley, was the grandmother of that Rebecca Townsend who became the first wife of Professor John Winthrop, LL. D., of Harvard College. As Rebecca Chamberlain figured in the delusions of witchcraft, her sister reappears in the wills and deeds recorded in Suffolk County. She was a beneficiary by the will of James Penn, Beadle to Governor John Winthrop in 1630, Messenger of Court and Ruling Elder of the First Church of Boston. She was also remembered in the will of Mrs. Anne Leverett, widow of Thomas Leverett, also a Ruling Elder of the First Church of Boston, and the mother of Sir John Leverett, Knt. and Governor of Massachusetts Bay from 1673 to 1679.

Would not those fifty members of this Association whose descent is traced from Rebecca Chamberlain, the gentlewoman, delight to unroll the parchment and discover the true significance of the words "my cousin" and "my kinsman" as legally used in 1687? Would not one little word relate us clearly on the maternal side to the Addingtons or the Leveretts of Old England and of New England?

Special investigation for individual members has been successfully carried on during the year. Of the ten individual investigations authorized by as many members, the Bureau has determined the Chamberlain ancestors of eight of these, carrying each member back to the progenitor. Along with these eight, twenty other members have been unconsciously carried to their progenitors.

These ancestral problems required of the Bureau absolutely accurate results from a variety of conditions and localities. Quite a year passed before we could find the antecedents of Joseph Chamberlain of Sunderland, Mass. Joshua Chamberlain of Westboro and Boston, Mass., was more easily affiliated. Again we unrolled the curtain behind

Jacob Chamberlain of Dudley, Mass. Ithamar Chamberlain of Oxford, Mass., was another. Then we were called to give the ancestors of the second John Chamberlain of Charlestown, Mass. William Chamberlin, of Hebron, Conn., made puzzling by the fact that Hebron contained two distinct families of our surname, was ancestered. One of the most interesting problems of the year was found in determining the forebears of *Jehu* Chamberlin of Spencertown, N. Y. A most critical examination of original records showed that two local historians had published his birth and marriage under the name *John* Chamberlain.

The difficulties surrounding the study of one's early ancestors are many. We are in constant confusion from published errors in local histories and family genealogies. We frequently find that the town or church records that we need to examine have been destroyed by fire or lost by carelessness. Many families in many towns in early times were so unfortunate as to fail of having their family records recorded among the vital statistics of the town. Many old records have faded and returned to the dust. Descendants often rely upon treacherous memory, dimmed by the lapse of time, which starts by locating the place of the birth of their grandfather, perhaps, miles from his native home, where perchance he lived some time later in life.

A friend of mine has been searching for months past to find the antecedents of a certain Carlton-Chamberlain family, supposed to have been born in the vicinity of Bangor, Maine. Within ten days of this writing, I accidentally discovered that about one hundred years ago, these identical parties were married in Southboro, Massachusetts, a distance of nearly two hundred and seventy-five miles from my friend's starting point.

Through the kindness of Mrs. Abbie Chamberlain Brant, of East Weymouth, Massachusetts, the Bureau has been permitted to copy a valuable collection of original letters written by, and relating to, the Rochester, New Hampshire, Chamberlains. Among these is a brief account of the capture by Indians, in 1776, of the great-grandfather of our honored president, and of our vice-president, General Samuel Emery Chamberlain. From Mrs. O. A. Furst, of Bellefonte, Pennsylvania, we have received valuable printed copies of the family records of Colonel William Chamberlain (1736–1817). Our Corresponding Secretary has rendered valuable assistance on the lines closely connected with her own.

The special investigation carried on by the Bureau have resulted in some important changes this year concerning the ancestry of our members.

Since our last report we have traced members as follows :

16 to Henry Chamberlin, of Hingham, 1638.

3 to Richard Chamberlin, of Braintree, 1642.

2 to Edmund Chamberlain, of Woburn, 1646.

7 to William Chamberlain, of Woburn, 1648.

3 to Jacob Chamberlain, of Rumney Marsh, 1720.

Our unancestored list has decreased by 17 and our miscellaneous list has decreased by 7.

As our membership now stands the Bureau traces :

16 to Henry Chamberlin, Hingham, 1638.

7 to Richard Chamberlin, Braintree, 1642.

3 to Thomas Chamberlain, Woburn, 1644.

8 to Edmund Chamberlain, 1646.

54 to William Chamberlain, Woburn, 1648.

14 to Jacob Chamberlain, Rumney Marsh, 1720.

10 to Lewis Chamberlin, of Flemington, N.J., about 1735.

3 to Samuel Chamberlaine, of Maryland, about 1735.

60 to various apparently disconnected branches.

43 to nobody.

19 associate members.

There are many lines yet resting in obscurity.

What were the antecedents of Jacob Chamberlain, of Rumney Marsh (now Revere), Massachusetts? More than a dozen prominent members would like to know.

What progenitor was Ephraim Chamberlain, of Northfield, Massachusetts, in 1730, descended from? This question concerns about a half-dozen members.

Several members would like to know the antecedents of Eliakim Chamberlain, of Dudley, Massachusetts.

Others call for the forebears of Ichabod Chamberlain, of Newburyport, Massachusetts; of Benjamin Chamberlain, of Winchendon, Massachusetts; of William Chamberlin, of Litchfield, Connecticut; of Joseph Chamberlain, of Tolland, Connecticut; of John Chamberlin, of Thetford, Vermont; of William Chamberlin, of Dunkirk, New York; of Ephraim Chamberlain, of Dalton, Massachusetts; of Peleg Chamberlain, of Kent, Connecticut, besides calls for ancestral lines in both England and Ireland.

These inquiries cannot be answered without making careful investigations of the records of various localities, and as many of the descendants of the names given have shown strength and attained distinction, we may feel assured that their ancestry was not ignoble — nay, that their progenitors lived worthily amid the conflicting political and religious claims of colonial life.

In conclusion, let me remind you that the study of one's ancestry brings to such an one nobler purposes in living, and reverence for the aged. With a learned Oxford professor let us remember that the " roots of the present lie deep in the past, and nothing in the past is dead to the man who would learn how the present comes to be what it is."

GEORGE W. CHAMBERLAIN,

Bureau Secretary.

TREASURER'S REPORT.

THOMAS CHAMBERLAIN, *Treasurer,*

In account with THE CHAMBERLAIN ASSOCIATION.

To amount received from the Assistant Treasurer,

October, 1898 . .	$25.00	
October, 1899 . .	25.00	
August, 1901	25.00	$75.00

BOSTON, September, 1901.

MISS SOPHIA A. CASWELL, *Assistant Treasurer*,

In account with THE CHAMBERLAIN ASSOCIATION.

Dr.

1900

Sept.	Balance on hand	$140.57
	Membership fees	201.00
	New members	17.00
	One Life Member . . .	25.00
	Subscription . . .	.60
	Sale of Reports . .	6.05 $390.22

Cr.

1900

Sept.	25.	Banquet deficit	$12.67
Oct.	13.	Miss A. F. Grant, printing 1000	
		Constitutions and By-Laws . .	15.00
		Express	.15
Oct.	14.	Oliver B. Graves, printing 600	
		Reports	70.00
Oct.	29.	Ida Lewis White, mimeographing	
		circulars	2.50
July	11.	Brown & Co., printing 300 circulars	2.50
		Assistant Treasurer Book . .	1.50
		P. O. Box (6 months) . . .	.50
		Postage, envelopes, paper, etc .	33.90
		Collection on checks . . .	1.70
		Paid Treasurer	25.00
		Balance on hand August 28, 1901 .	224.80 $390.22

September, 1901.

OFFICERS FOR THE CURRENT YEAR.

President.

MAJ.-GEN. JOSHUA L. CHAMBERLAIN, LL D.,
Brunswick, Me.

Vice-Presidents.

HON. DANIEL H. CHAMBERLAIN, LL. D.,
West Brookfield, Mass.

BRIG.-GEN. SAMUEL E. CHAMBERLAIN,
Barre, Mass.

COL. THOMAS CHAMBERLIN,
Philadelphia, Pa.

REV. E. E. STRONG, D. D.,
Boston, Mass.

PROF. T. C. CHAMBERLIN, LL. D.,
Chicago, Ill.

MYRON L. CHAMBERLAIN, M. D.,
Boston, Mass.

COL. SIMON E. CHAMBERLIN,
Washington, D. C.

COL. HENRY H. ADAMS,
New York.

MR. L. H. CHAMBERLIN,
Detroit, Mich.

PRES. McKENDREE H. CHAMBERLAIN, LL D.,
Lebanon, Ill.

CAPT. A. P. ANDREW,
La Porte, Ind.

Corresponding Secretary.

MISS ABBIE M. CHAMBERLAIN,
>Washington, D. C., and
>Box 218, Braintree, Mass.

Recording Secretary.

MR. ASA W. CHAMBERLIN,
>Jamaica Plain, Mass.

Treasurer.

MR. THOMAS CHAMBERLAIN,
>State National Bank, Boston.

Assistant Treasurer.

MRS. SOPHIA A. CHAMBERLAIN CASWELL,
>27 River Street, Cambridgeport, Mass.

Additional Members of Executive Committee.

MISS LAURA B. CHAMBERLAIN,
>Washington, D. C.

MR. MONTAGUE CHAMBERLAIN,
>Cambridge, Mass.

MR. THOMAS E. CHAMBERLIN,
>Brookline, Mass.

STANDING COMMITTEES.

Genealogical Committee.

MR. JACOB CHESTER CHAMBERLAIN, *Chairman*,
1 W. 81st Street, New York.

REV. LEANDER T. CHAMBERLAIN, D. D.,
New York.

COL. THOMAS CHAMBERLIN,
Philadelphia, Pa.

MR. HERBERT B. CHAMBERLAIN,
Brattleboro, Vt.

G. M. CHAMBERLIN, M. D.,
Chicago, Ill.

MISS JENNIE CHAMBERLAIN WATTS,
Cambridge, Mass.

MISS ISABELLA S. CHAMBERLIN,
Washington, D. C.

Committee on Colonial and American Revolutionary History.

J. W. CHAMBERLIN, M. D., *Chairman*.
Endicott Building, St. Paul, Minn.

MR. WILLIAM S. BOYNTON,
St. Johnsbury, Vt.

MRS. H. H. BURNHAM,
Putnam, Conn.

PROF. PAUL MELLEN CHAMBERLAIN,
Chicago, Ill.

MRS. O. A. FURST,
Bellefonte, Pa.

MISS S. EMMA CHAMBERLIN,
Cleveland, O.

MR. PRESCOTT CHAMBERLAIN,
Boston, Mass.

Committee on English Ancestry.

REV. LEANDER T. CHAMBERLAIN, D. D., *Chairman,*
The Chelsea, New York.

MR. JOHN WILSON CHAMBERLAIN,
Tiffin, O.

MRS. HARRIET P. KIMBALL,
Dubuque, Iowa.

MR. JOHN C. ORDWAY,
Concord, N. H.

MR. HENRY R. CHAMBERLAIN,
London, England.

Committee on Recent Wars.

CAPT. ORVILLE T. CHAMBERLAIN, *Chairman,*
Elkhart, Ind.

GENERAL FRANK CHAMBERLAIN,
Albany, N. Y.

MR. ROLLIN S. CHAMBERLIN,
Wilkes Barre, Pa.

MR. DWIGHT S. CHAMBERLAIN,
Lyons, N. Y.

MRS. EMILY A. CAPRON,
Winchendon, Mass.

MISS HELEN C. CHAMBERLAIN,
Washington, D. C.

MRS. ELLEN E. C. BLAIR,
Dorchester, Mass.

LIST OF MEMBERS.

(Those in heavy-faced type are "charter" members; those marked with an asterisk are dead.)

Active Members.

COL. HENRY H. ADAMS,	New York, N. Y.
CAPT. A. P. ANDREW,	La Porte, Ind.
MRS. MARTHA E. AUSTIN,	Roxbury, Mass.
MRS. E. S. BARTLETT,	Evanston, Ill.
MRS. ELLEN E. C. BLAIR,	Dorchester, Mass.
MISS AMY E. BLANCHARD,	Philadelphia, Pa.
*MR. D. C. BLOOMER,	Council Bluffs, Iowa.
(Died February 26, 1900.	
MRS. S. M. BODWELL,	Clifton Springs, N. Y.
MR. WILLIAM S. BOYNTON,	St. Johnsbury, Vt.
MRS. J. M. BRANT,	East Weymouth, Mass.
MRS. GEORGE M. BROWN,	Hartford, Conn.
MRS. J. S. BROWNE,	La Grange, Ind.
MRS. MARY C. BURNHAM,	Putnam, Conn.
MRS. CARRIE M. BUTTS,	Newton Centre, Mass.
MRS. EMILY A. CAPRON,	Winchendon, Mass.
MRS. SOPHIA A. C. CASWELL,	Cambridgeport, Mass.
MISS ABBIE M. CHAMBERLAIN,	Washington, D. C.

MR. A. C. ALLEN CHAMBERLAIN,	Winchester. Mass.
MISS ALICE CHAMBERLAIN,	Hyde Park, Mass.
MR. ALLEN CHAMBERLIN,	New York, N. Y.
MR. ALLEN G. CHAMBERLAIN.	Idaho Springs, Col.
ALLEN H. CHAMBERLAIN, M. D.,	Foxcroft, Me.
MISS ANNA P. CHAMBERLAIN,	East Orange, N. J.
MR. ANSEL E. CHAMBERLIN,	Dalton, Mass.
MR. ARTHUR B. CHAMBERLAIN,	Rochester, N. Y.
MR. ALBERT S. CHAMBERLIN.	Hartford, Conn.
MR. ASA W. CHAMBERLIN,	Jamaica Plain, Mass.
MR. BURR C. CHAMBERLIN,	Dalton, Mass.
MISS CATHERINE J. CHAMBERLAYNE,	Boston, Mass.
MR. CECIL C. CHAMBERLAIN,	Enderlin, North Dakota.
MR. CHARLES A. CHAMBERLIN,	Detroit, Mich.
MR. CHARLES A. CHAMBERLIN,	Westford, Mass.
MR. CHARLES E. CHAMBERLIN,	Roxbury, Mass.
MR. CHARLES H. CHAMBERLIN,	Dalton, Mass.
MR. CHARLES H. CHAMBERLIN,	Kingston, Pa.
*MR. CHARLES K. CHAMBERLIN,	Pittsburgh, Pa.
(Died May 14, 1899.)	
MR. CHARLES T. CHAMBERLAIN,	Minneapolis, Minn.
MR. CLARK W. CHAMBERLAIN,	La Grange, Ohio.
*CYRUS N. CHAMBERLAIN, M. D.,	Andover, Mass.
(Died July 18, 1899.)	
MR. CHARLES W. CHAMBERLAIN,	Dayton, Ohio.
MR. CHAUNCY W. CHAMBERLAIN,	Boston, Mass.
MR. CLARENCE M. CHAMBERLAIN,	Rochester, N. Y.

HON. DANIEL H. CHAMBERLAIN, LL. D.,
West Brookfield, Mass.

*HON. DANIEL U. CHAMBERLIN, Cambridgeport, Mass.
(Died June 15, 1898.)

MISS DELIA CARA CHAMBERLIN, Burlington, Iowa.

MR. DWIGHT S. CHAMBERLAIN, Lyons, N. Y.

MR. EDWARD WILLMOT CHAMBERLAIN, New York, N. Y.

MR. EDWARD WATTS CHAMBERLAIN, Louisville, Ky.

MR. EDWIN A. CHAMBERLIN, Trenton, N. J.

EDWIN C. CHAMBERLIN, M. D., New York, N. Y.

MISS ELISABETH CHAMBERLIN, Torresdale, Pa.

MISS ELISABETH E. CHAMBERLAIN, Providence, R. I.

MISS ELLA J. CHAMBERLAIN, Cambridge, Mass.

MR. EPHRAIM CHAMBERLAIN, Medfield, Mass.

MR. ERNEST V. CHAMBERLIN, Cincinnati, Ohio.

MR. EUGENE G. CHAMBERLIN. Chicago, Ill.

MR. EUGENE TYLER CHAMBERLAIN, Washington, D. C.

GEN. FRANK CHAMBERLAIN, Albany, N. Y.

MR. FRANK D. CHAMBERLAIN, Columbus, Ohio.

MR. FRANK E. CHAMBERLAIN, Manistee, Mich.

MR. FRANK H. CHAMBERLAIN, Hudson, Mass.

MR. FREDERIC E. CHAMBERLIN. Bayonne, N. J.

MR. FRED W. CHAMBERLIN, Detroit, Mich.

MR. FRANK D. CHAMBERLIN, Hartford, Conn.

MR. F. W. CHAMBERLAIN, Three Oaks, Mich.

MR. GEORGE B. CHAMBERLIN, Chicago, Ill.

MR. GEORGE F. CHAMBERLIN, New York, N. Y.

MR. G. HOWARD CHAMBERLIN,	Yonkers, N. Y.
MR. GEORGE M. CHAMBERLIN, M. D.,	Chicago, Ill.
MR. GEORGE R. CHAMBERLAIN,	New Haven, Conn.
REV. GEO. U. CHAMBERLAIN, D. D.,	Bahia, Brazil, S. A.
MR. GEORGE W. CHAMBERLAIN,	Weymouth, Mass.
MR. GEO. THOMAS CHAMBERLAIN,	Columbus, Ohio.
MISS GERTRUDE CHAMBERLIN,	Boston, Mass.
MR. HARLOW H. CHAMBERLAIN,	Minneapolis Minn.
MR. HARRY G. CHAMBERLIN,	Chicago, Ill.
MISS HELEN CHAMBERLAIN,	Hyde Park, Mass.
MISS HELEN M. C. CHAMBERLAIN,	Washington, D. C.
MISS HENRIETTA M. CHAMBERLAINE,	Baltimore, Md.
MR. HENRY CHAMBERLAIN,	Three Oaks, Mich.
MR. HENRY E. CHAMBERLIN,	Gridley, Kan.
MR. HENRY L. CHAMBERLIN,	Buffalo, N. Y.
MR. HENRY N. CHAMBERLAIN,	Chicago, Ill.
MR. HENRY R. CHAMBERLAIN,	London, England.
MR. HERBERT B. CHAMBERLIN,	Brattleboro, Vt.
MR. HIRAM S. CHAMBERLAIN,	Chattanooga, Tenn.
MR. HORACE P. CHAMBERLAIN,	Buffalo, N. Y.
MR. I. C. CHAMBERLAIN,	Dubuque, Iowa.
MISS ISABELLA S. CHAMBERLIN,	Washington, D. C
REV. JACOB CHAMBERLAIN, D. D.,	Madanapalle, Ind.
MR. JACOB A. CHAMBERLAIN,	Warwick, N. Y.
MR. JACOB CHESTER CHAMBERLAIN,	New York, N. Y.
REV. JAMES A. CHAMBERLIN, D. D.,	Torrington, Conn.

43

MR. JAMES F. CHAMBERLAIN,	Los Angeles, Cal.
MR. JAMES ROSWELL CHAMBERLIN,	Rochester, N. Y.
MR. JAMES W. CHAMBERLAIN,	Akron, Ohio.
MISS JESSIE C. CHAMBERLIN,	Boston, Mass.
MR. JOHN CHAMBERLIN,	Lexington, Mo.
MR. JOHN C. CHAMBERLIN,	Dalton, Mass.
MR. JOHN F. CHAMBERLIN,	Summit, N. J.
MR. JOHN W. CHAMBERLAIN,	Portland, Or.
MR. JOHN WILSON CHAMBERLIN,	Tiffin, Ohio.
*JOSEPH E. M. CHAMBERLAIN, M. D.,	Easton, Md.
(Died January 30, 1901.)	
MR. JOS. EDGAR CHAMBERLAIN,	New York.
* MR. JOS. L. CHAMBERLAIN,	Cherry Valley, N. Y.
(Died December 30, 1900).	
MAJ.-GEN. JOSHUA L. CHAMBERLAIN, LL. D.,	
	Brunswick, Me.
MR. J. D. CHAMBERLIN,	Toledo, Ohio.
MR. J. H. CHAMBERLIN,	Chicago, Ill.
J. P. CHAMBERLIN, M. D.,	Boston, Mass.
MR. J. R. CHAMBERLAIN,	Raleigh, N. C.
J. W. CHAMBERLIN, M. D.,	St. Paul, Minn.
MISS LAURA B. CHAMBERLAIN,	Cambridge, Mass.
MR. LEON T. CHAMBERLAIN,	St. Paul, Minn.
MR. LEWIS H. CHAMBERLAIN,	Detroit, Mich.
MISS LIZZIE F. CHAMBERLAIN,	Cambridge, Mass.
HON. LLOYD E. CHAMBERLIN,	Brockton, Mass.
MARK CHAMBERLIN, LL. D.,	Cody, Wyo.

MARK A. CHAMBERLAIN, M. D.,   Winthrop, Iowa.

MR. MARTIN H. CHAMBERLIN,   Rutland, Vt.

MISS MARY CHAMBERLIN,   Torresdale, Pa.

MISS MARY DUNTON CHAMBERLAIN,   Roxbury, Mass.

PRES. McKENDREE H. CHAMBERLIN, LL. D., Lebanon, Ill.

* **HON. MELLEN CHAMBERLAIN, LL. D.**, Chelsea, Mass.
(Died June 25, 1900.)

MR. MONTAGUE CHAMBERLAIN,   Cambridge, Mass.

MR. MOSES CHAMBERLIN,   Milton, Pa.

MYRON L. CHAMBERLAIN, M. D.,   Boston, Mass.

MR. NAHUM B. CHAMBERLAIN,   Jamaica Plain, Mass.

MR. NEWELL CHAMBERLAIN,   Cambridge, Mass.

MR. NORMAN A. CHAMBERLAIN,   Charleston, S. C.

* **MISS N. AUGUSTA CHAMBERLAIN,** Auburndale, Mass.
(Died March 22, 1900.)

* REV. N. H. CHAMBERLAYNE,   Monument Beach, Mass.
(Died April 1, 1901.)

MR. OREN S. CHAMBERLAIN,   Chicago, Ill.

CAPT. ORVILLE T. CHAMBERLAIN,   Elkhart, Ind.

MR. PATRICK CHAMBERLAINE,   Chicago, Ill.

PROF. PAUL MELLEN CHAMBERLAIN,   Chicago, Ill.

MR. PRESCOTT CHABERLAIN,   Chelsea, Mass.

MR. RICHARD H. CHAMBERLAIN,   Oakland, Cal.

GEN. ROBERT H. CHAMBERLAIN,   Worcester, Mass.

MR. ROLLIN S. CHAMBERLIN,   Wilkesbarre, Pa.

MR. ROSWELL W. CHAMBERLAIN,   Chester, N. Y.

BRIG.-GEN. SAMUEL E. CHAMBERLAIN,
Barre Plain, Mass.

MISS SARAH P. CHAMBERLAIN,   Salem, Mass.

MR. SIMEON E. CHAMBERLAIN,	Kansas City, Mo.
MR. SYLVESTER CHAMBERLAIN,	Buffalo, N. Y.
COL. SIMON E. CHAMBERLIN,	Washington, D. C.
MISS S. EMMA CHAMBERLIN,	Cleveland, Ohio.
MR. SAMUEL D. CHAMBERLIN,	Hartford, Conn.
MR. S. R. CHAMBERLAIN,	Chicago, Ill.
MR. S. T. CHAMBERLIN.	Derby, Conn.
MR. STILLMAN W. CHAMBERLIN.	Braintree, Mass.
PROF. T. C. CHAMBERLIN, LL. D.,	Chicago, Ill.
COL. THOMAS CHAMBERLIN,	Philadelphia, Pa.
MR. THOMAS CHAMBERLAIN,	Hyde Park, Mass.
MR. THOMAS E. CHAMBERLIN,	Brookline, Mass.
MR. WARD B. CHAMBERLIN,	New York, N. Y.
MR. WARREN CHAMBERLAIN,	Honolulu, H. I.
MR. WILBUR F. CHAMBERLAIN,	Hannibal, Mo.
MR. WILLARD DeWITT CHAMBERLIN,	Dayton, Ohio.
MR. WILLARD CHAMBERLAIN,	Watertown, Mass.
MR. WILLIAM CHAMBERLAIN,	Portland, Me.
PROF. WILLIAM B. CHAMBERLAIN,	Oak Park, Ill.
MR. WILLIAM B. CHAMBERLIN,	Torresdale, Pa.
MR. WILLIAM C. CHAMBERLAIN,	Charlottesville, Va.
MR. WILLIAM C. CHAMBERLAIN,	Dubuque, Iowa.
MR. WILLIAM CARLTON CHAMBERLAIN,	Louisville, Ky.
MR. WILLIAM H. CHAMBERLIN,	Chicago, Ill.
MR. WILLIAM H. CHAMBERLIN,	Cincinnati, Ohio.
MR. WILLIAM H. CHAMBERLAIN,	Kanona, N. Y.

MR. WILLIAM JOSEPH CHAMBERLAIN,	Denver, Col.
*MR. WILLIAM N. CHAMBERLIN,	Pittsfield, Mass.
(Died August 9, 1901.)	
MAJOR WILLIAM N. CHAMBERLIN,	Washington, D. C.
MR. WILLIAM PORTER CHAMBERLAIN,	Knoxville, Tenn.
MR. WILLIAM S. CHAMBERLAIN,	Cleveland, Ohio.
MRS. T. EATON CLAPP,	Albany, N. Y.
MR. ALBERT CHAMBERLAIN CLARKE,	Southbridge, Mass.
*MRS. ALICE G. CHAMBERLAIN CLARKE,	
(Died July 8, 1899).	Southbridge, Mass.
MRS. MARY L. C. CLARKE,	Andover, Mass.
MRS. ALFRED W. COLE,	Boston, Mass.
EDWARD COWLES, M. D.,	Waverley, Mass.
MRS. CROYDON CRAIN,	Jamaica Plain, Mass.
MRS. T. W. DALE,	Auburndale, Mass.
MRS. AMIE WHITING DAMON,	Reading, Mass.
MRS. NATHAN A. DAVIS.	Concord, Mass.
MRS. A. E. DICK,	Andover, Mass.
MRS. KATE C. DILLINGHAM,	Denver, Col.
MRS. SARAH C. ECCLESTON.	Buenos Aires.
MR. CHARLES N. FESSENDEN,	Chicago, Ill.
JUDGE WILLIAM T. FORBES,	Worcester, Mass.
MISS HARRIOTT A. FOX,	Chicago, Ill.
MRS. CAROLINE W. FURST,	Bellefonte. Pa.
MISS M. E. GROVER,	White River Junction, Vt.
MRS. HELEN GUILFORD,	Minneapolis, Minn.
MRS. O. H. HARDING,	Allston, Mass.

MRS. LUCY CHAMBERLAIN HAYWARD, London, Eng.

MRS. HARRIET C. I. HEWITT, Saratoga Springs, N. Y.

MISS LOUISE H. HINCKLEY, Cambridge, Mass.

MISS LIDA HOOPER, New York City, N.Y.

MRS. H. T. C. HUGHES, Mobile, Ala.

MRS. CLEORA E. JEFFERDS, Foxcroft, Me.

MISS CHARLOTTE A. JEWELL, Hartford, Conn.

MRS. ANNIE B. CHAMBERLAIN KEENE, Woodfords, Me.

MRS. ETTA F. C. KENDALL, Auburndale, Mass.

MRS. ELIZA M. C. KENNEDY, Watertown, Mass.

MR. HORACE KENNEDY, Watertown, Mass.

MRS. J. L. KENT, Everett, Mass.

MRS. HARRIET P. KIMBALL, Dubuque, Iowa.

MRS. J. H. LIGHT, Bloomington, Ill.

MRS. HELEN M. C. LLOYD, Chicago, Ill.

MRS. C. B. McLEAN, Pittsburgh, Pa.

REV. MOSES MARTIN, D. D., Ovid, Mich.

MRS. JAMES A. MERRITT, Baltimore, Md.

MRS. FLORENCE CHAMBERLAIN MOSELEY,
New Haven, Conn.

MR. JOHN CHAMBERLAIN ORDWAY, Concord, N. H.

MRS. CARRIE A. C. OXFORD, Cambridge, Mass.

MR. GEORGE HERBERT PERRY, Cambridge, Mass.

MRS. MINNIE A. C. PERRY, Cambridge, Mass.

MR. RALPH DANA PERRY, Cambridge, Mass.

MRS. CHARLES B. PLATT, Englewood, N. J.

MRS. ARTHUR H. PRAY, Boston, Mass.

MR. JOHN S. RINGWALT, JR.,	Mt. Vernon, Ohio.
MR. RALPH CURTIS RINGWALT,	Mt. Vernon, Ohio.
MRS. ALBERT S. ROE,	New York, N. Y.
MISS EMMA TEN-BROECK RUNK,	Lambertville, N. J.
MRS. C. W. SEYMOUR,	Hingham, Mass.
MRS. ANNA EUGENIA SMILEY,	Marblehead, Mass.
MR. ARTHUR C. SPRAGUE,	Wollaston, Mass.
MR. FRANK H. SPRAGUE,	Wollaston, Mass.
REV. E. E. STRONG, D. D.,	Auburndale, Mass.
MISS JENNIE CHAMBERLAIN WATTS,	Cambridge, Mass.
MRS. MARTHA C. WILSON,	Woodfords, Me.

ASSOCIATE MEMBERS.

MR. GEORGE M. BROWN,	Hartford, Conn.
MR. GEORGE B. CASWELL,	Cambridgeport, Mass.
MISS ALICE RHEA CHAMBERLIN,	Torresdale, Pa.
MRS. ANNA GARLAND CHAMBERLAIN,	Andover, Mass.
MRS. ASA W. CHAMBERLIN,	Jamaica Plain, Mass.
MRS. CATHERINE W. CHAMBERLAIN,	Cambridge, Mass.
MRS. EMMA B. CHAMBERLIN,	Chicago, Ill.
MRS. EUGENE G. CHAMBERLIN,	Chicago, Ill.
MRS. FANNIE E. CHAMBERLIN,	Philadelphia, Pa.
MRS. JACOB C. CHAMBERLAIN,	New York, N. Y.
MRS. M. A. CHAMBERLIN,	Greenville, N. H.

MRS. NEWELL CHAMBERLAIN,	Cambridge, Mass.
MRS. ROBERT H. CHAMBERLAIN,	Worcester, Mass.
MRS. SAMUEL E. CHAMBERLAIN,	Barre Plain, Mass.
MRS. THOMAS CHAMBERLAIN,	Hyde Park, Mass.
MR. CHARLES DAMON,	Reading, Mass.
MR. NATHAN A. DAVIS,	Concord, Mass.
MR. JAMES H. KENDALL,	Auburndale, Mass.
MR. OSCAR H. LELAND,	Springfield, Vt.
MR. FRANK W. PERRY,	Cambridge, Mass.
(Died June 20, 1898.)	
MRS. WILLARD CHAMBERLAIN,	Watertown, Mass.

LIFE MEMBERS.

MRS. LUCY P. CHAMBERLAIN,	Medford, Mass.
REV. L. T. CHAMBERLAIN, LL.D.,	New York City, N. Y.
MR. WM. CHAMBERLAIN,	West Chesterfield, N. H.

www.ingramcontent.com/pod-product-compliance
Lightning Source LLC
Chambersburg PA
CBHW030312270326
41926CB00010B/1328